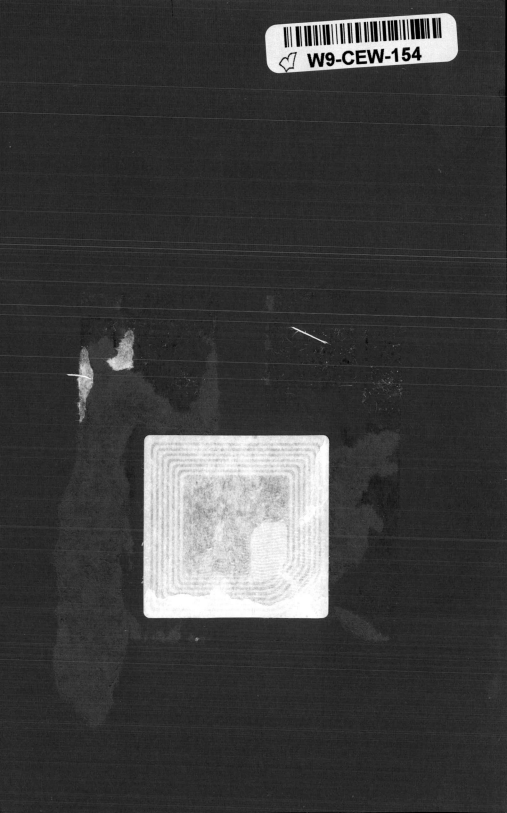

Great Sayings

GREAT SAYINGS

Classic Words from Modern Times

OVERLOOK DUCKWORTH

New York • London

This edition first published in hardcover in the United States in 2012 by
The Overlook Press, Peter Mayer Publishers, Inc.

NEW YORK
141 Wooster Street
New York, NY 10012
www.overlookpress.com
For bulk and special sales please contact sales@overlookny.com

LONDON
90-93 Cowcross Street
London EC1M 6BF
inquiries@duckworth-publishers.co.uk
www.ducknet.co.uk

Compiled by Gertrud Watson, Matthew Sims, Helen Golding and Jane Evans.
Page design by Crispin Goodall

Cataloging-in-Publication Data is available from the Library of Congress

Printed in the United States of America

1 3 5 7 9 8 6 4 2

ISBN (US) 978-1-4683-0047-5

ISBN (UK) 978-0-7156-4152-1

Contents

Love,
Sex and
Marriage

If you would be loved, love and be loveable.
BENJAMIN FRANKLIN, *Poor Richard's Almanack*

Women love us for our faults. If we have enough of them, they will forgive us everything, even our intellects.
OSCAR WILDE, *The Picture of Dorian Gray*

Love has its own dark morality when rivalry enters in.
THOMAS HARDY, *Jude the Obscure*

If thou rememberest not the slightest folly
That ever love did make thee run into
Thou hast not loved.
WILLIAM SHAKESPEARE, *As You Like It*

It's not the seven deadly virtues that make a man a good husband, but the three hundred pleasing amiabilities.
SOMERSET MAUGHAM, Attrib.

She respected her husband in the same way as she respected the General Post Office, as something large, secure and fixed; and though she knew the small number of his talents she appreciated his abstract value as a male.
JAMES JOYCE, *Dubliners*

Men are given to the trick of having a passing fancy for somebody else in the midst of permanent love, which reasserts itself afterwards just as before.
THOMAS HARDY, *A Pair of Blue Eyes*

Love stretches hands from shore to shore:
Love is, and shall not perish!
LEWIS CARROLL, *Life and Letters*

Marriage – yes, it is the supreme felicity of life. I concede it. And it is also the supreme tragedy of life. The deeper the love the surer the tragedy. And the more disconsolating when it comes.
MARK TWAIN, *Letters*

That illusion of young romantic love to which women look
forever forward and forever back.
F. SCOTT FITZGERALD, *The Beautiful and Damned*

Idleness which is often becoming and even wise in the bachelor, begins to wear a different aspect when you have a wife to support.
ROBERT LOUIS STEVENSON, *Virginibus Puerisque*

Single women have a dreadful propensity for being poor – which is one very strong argument in favour of matrimony.
JANE AUSTEN, *Letters*, 13 March 1817

Talk not of love, it gives me pain,
For love has been my foe;
He bound me in an iron chain,
And plunged me deep in woe.

ROBERT BURNS, 'Love in the Guise of Friendship'

To church in the morning, and there saw a wedding in the
church, which I have not seen many a day, and the young
people so merry one with another; and strange, to see what
delight we married people have to see these poor fools
decoyed into our condition, every man and wife
gazing and smiling at them.

SAMUEL PEPYS, *The Diary of Samuel Pepys*, Christmas Day 1665

Love is stronger than Cruelty, stronger than Death, but
perishes under Meanness; Pity may take
its place, but Pity is not Love.

CHARLOTTE BRONTË, Letter to W.S. Williams, 1 May 1848

Only in gentle opposition like a well drilled spouse.

SIR WALTER SCOTT, *The Journal of Sir Walter Scott*

Nothing spoils romance so much as a sense of humour in
the woman.

OSCAR WILDE, *A Woman of No Importance*

Lord Shelburne used to say that perfect society was wives
without husbands and husbands without wives.

BENJAMIN DISRAELI, *Disraeli's Reminiscences*

I don't love anyone except my family.
JAMES JOYCE, Attrib.

A wedding is a licensed subject to joke upon, but there really
is no great joke in the matter after all.
CHARLES DICKENS, *The Pickwick Papers*

Love frequently dies of time alone – much more frequently
of displacement.
THOMAS HARDY, *A Pair of Blue Eyes*

Love is based on inequality as friendship is on equality.
W. B. YEATS, *John Sherman*

It is very hard sometimes to know how intensely we are loved,
and of what value our presence is to those who love us.
ANTHONY TROLLOPE, *Last Chronicle of Barset*

Love can't give any man new gifts. It can only heighten the
gifts he was born with.
GEORGE BERNARD SHAW, *You Can Never Tell*

The true love story commences at the alter, when there lies
before the married pair a most beautiful contest of
wisdom and generosity, and a life-long struggle towards the
unattainable ideal.
ROBERT LOUIS STEVENSON, 'El Dorado'

'Nobody, who has not been in the interior of a family, can say what the difficulties of any individual of that family may be.'
JANE AUSTEN, *Emma* (Emma Woodhouse)

There are all kinds of love in the world, but never the same love twice.
F. SCOTT FITZGERALD, 'The Sensible Thing'

[Quizzed by American reporters on rumours he was to marry]
People just can't bear to see me being
a happy and unmolested bachelor.
NOËL COWARD, New York News, 1937

The happiness of a married man ... depends on the people he has not married.
OSCAR WILDE, *A Woman of No Importance*

Qualities that make a good husband: an agreeable temper, a sense of humour and an entire indifference to petty extravagance.
SOMERSET MAUGHAM, Attrib.

By the time you swear you're his,
Shivering and sighing,
And he vows his passion is
Infinite, undying –
Lady, make a note of this:
One of you is lying.
DOROTHY PARKER, 'Unfortunate Coincidence'

The course of true love never did run smooth.
WILLIAM SHAKESPEARE, *A Midsummer Night's Dream*

Love is faith.
THOMAS HARDY, *A Pair of Blue Eyes*

Gentle lady, do not sing
Sad songs about the end of love;
Lay aside sadness and sing
How love that passes is enough.
JAMES JOYCE, *Chamber Music*

To know and love one other human being
is the root of all wisdom.
EVELYN WAUGH, *Brideshead Revisited*

Where there's marriage without love there will be
love without marriage.
BENJAMIN FRANKLIN, *Poor Richard's Almanack*

Venus, a beautiful good-natur'd lady, was the Goddess of Love;
Juno, a terrible shrew, the Goddess of Marriage; and
they were always mortal enemies.
JONATHAN SWIFT, *Thoughts on Various Subjects*

There is no love but love at first sight.
BENJAMIN DISRAELI, *Henrietta Temple*

I rather look upon love altogether as a sort of
hostile transaction, very necessary to make or
to break matches, and keep the world going, but by
no means a sinecure to the parties concerned.
Lord Byron, Letter to Lady Hardy, 1822

Love should run out to meet love with open arms.
Robert Louis Stevenson, 'El Dorado'

Most people live *for* love and admiration. But it is *by* love and
admiration that we should live. If any love is shown us we
should recognise that we are quite unworthy of it.
Oscar Wilde, *De Profundis*

A family of ten children will always be called a fine family,
where there are heads and arms and legs enough
for the number.
Jane Austen, *Northanger Abbey*

I am sure that no law made by man is sacred before the
impulse of passion.
James Joyce, *Exiles*

As for thinking that I should have exhorted you to go to
a marriage service, I can only say last time I went to
one I had much ado not to stand up and cry out on
the disgusting nature of it.
Virginia Woolf, Letter, 27 March 1937

It is a solemn and strange and perilous thing for a woman to become a wife.
CHARLOTTE BRONTË, Letter to Ellen Nussey, 9 August 1854

'Ven you're a married man, Samivel, you'll understand a good many things as you don't understand now; but vether it's worth while goin' through so much, to learn so little, as the charity-boy said ven he got to the end of the alphabet, is a matter o' taste. *I* rather think it isn't.'
CHARLES DICKENS, *The Pickwick Papers* (Tony Weller)

The love of an inconstant man is ten times more ardent than that of a faithful man – that is, while it lasts.
THOMAS HARDY, *Desperate Remedies*

Save in the very young, only love begets love.
F. SCOTT FITZGERALD, 'Josephine: A Woman with a Past'

Maids are May when they are maids, but the sky changes when they are wives.
WILLIAM SHAKESPEARE, *As You Like It*

Promising to love, honour and obey one's husband – the kind of undertaking no one is really expected to carry out.
SOMERSET MAUGHAM, Attrib.

For my own part I never had the least thought or
inclination of turning Poet till I got once heartily in love,
and then Rhyme and Song were, in a manner,
the spontaneous language of my heart.
ROBERT BURNS, *Journal*, August 1793

The truth is, perhaps, the lover's pleasure, like that of the
hunter, is in the chase; and that the brightest beauty loses half
its merit, as the fairest flower its perfume, when the willing
hand can reach it too easily.
SIR WALTER SCOTT, *Redgauntlet*

Love is fed by the imagination, by which we become wiser
than we know, better than we feel, nobler than we are:
by which we can see life as a whole: by which, and by which
alone, we can understand others in their real as in
their ideal relations.
OSCAR WILDE, *De Profundis*

You do not love another because he is wealthy or wise or
eminently respectable; you love him because you love him;
that is love ...
ROBERT LOUIS STEVENSON, 'Lay Morals'

Marriage, Sir is much more necessary to a man than
to a woman; for he is much less able to supply himself with
domestic comforts.
DR JOHNSON, Attrib.

When passion is dead, or absent, then the magnificent throb of beauty is incomprehensible and even a little despicable ... warm, live beauty of contact, so much deeper than the beauty of vision.
D. H. LAWRENCE, *Lady Chatterley's Lover*

Win me, woo me, wed me, ah weary me!
JAMES JOYCE, *Finnegans Wake*

You can't reason with your own heart; it has its own laws, and thumps about things which the intellect scorns.
MARK TWAIN, *Connecticut Yankee*

It seems to me that love, if fine, is essentially a discipline.
W. B. YEATS, *Journal*, January 1909

'There are very few of us who have heart enough to be really in love without encouragement.'
JANE AUSTEN, *Pride and Prejudice* (Charlotte Lucas)

There are two powers at which men should never grumble – the weather and their wives.
BENJAMIN DISRAELI, Attrib.

It is foreign to a man's nature to go on loving a person when he is told that he must and shall be that person's lover.
THOMAS HARDY, *Jude the Obscure*

Sorrow's a lot of fun for most women and
for some men, but it seems to me that a marriage
ought to be based on hope.
F. Scott Fitzgerald, 'The Bridal Party'

He that falls in love with Himself, will have no Rivals.
Benjamin Franklin, *Poor Richard's Almanack*

No married man is ever attractive except to his wife.
Oscar Wilde, *The Importance of Being Earnest*

There is comfort in the strength of love;
Twill make a thing endurable, which else
Would overset the brain, or break the heart.
William Wordsworth, 'Michael'

The ideal love affair is one conducted by post.
My correspondence with Ellen Terry was a wholly satisfactory
love affair ... She got tired of five husbands; but
she never got tired of me.
George Bernard Shaw, Letter to Hesketh Pearson

I consider boredom the most legitimate of
all reasons for a divorce.
Noël Coward, World Telegram, 1931

Marriage is terrifying, but so is a cold and forlorn old age.
Robert Louis Stevenson, *Virginibus Puerisque*

Never gamble at the game of life; be content to play for
sixpences; marriage is too high a stake for a wise man to risk.
SYDNEY SMITH, *Memoir*

Love is a cursed nuisance especially when
coupled with lust also.
JAMES JOYCE, Letter, 7 September 1909

Women dislike intelligence in husbands.
SOMERSET MAUGHAM, Attrib.

Matrimonial differences are usually discussed by the parties
concerned in the form of a dialogue, in which
the lady bears at least her full half share
CHARLES DICKENS, *Old Curiosity Shop*

Love is for unlucky folk,
Love is but a curse.
Once there was a heart I broke:
And that, I think, is worse
DOROTHY PARKER, *The Collected Dorothy Parker*

The enthusiasm of a woman's love is even
beyond the biographer's.
JANE AUSTEN, *Mansfield Park*

If Jack's in love, he's no judge of Jill's beauty.
BENJAMIN FRANKLIN, *Poor Richard's Almanack*

When a woman marries again it is because she detested her first husband. When a man marries again it is because he adored his first wife. Women try their luck; men risk theirs.
OSCAR WILDE, *The Picture of Dorian Gray*

The plainest person can look beautiful, can *be* beautiful. It only needs the fire of sex to rise delicately to change an ugly face to a lovely one.
D. H. LAWRENCE, 'Sex versus Loveliness'

Love is not love
Which alters when it alteration finds,
Or bends with the remover to remove.
WILLIAM SHAKESPEARE, Sonnet 116

'Millions of marriages are unhappy; if everybody confessed the truth, perhaps all are more or less so.'
CHARLOTTE BRONTË, *Shirley* (Mr Helstone)

And so, standing before the aforesaid officiator, the two swore that at every other time of their lives, they would assuredly believe, feel, and desire precisely as they had believed, felt and desired during the few preceding weeks. What was remarkable as the undertaking itself was the fact that nobody seemed at all surprised at what they swore.
THOMAS HARDY, *Jude the Obscure*

He was his wife's man and not his own.
F. SCOTT FITZGERALD, *The Beautiful and Damned*

What is life when wanting Love?
Night without a morning.
Love's the cloudless summer sun,
Nature gay adorning.
ROBERT BURNS, 'Thine Am I, My Faithful Fair'

She rules her husband, but that I suppose is always the case
when marriages are what is called happy [of Lady Lytton].
BENJAMIN DISRAELI, Letters

No woman should marry a teetotaller,
or a man who does not smoke.
ROBERT LOUIS STEVENSON, Virginibus Puerisque

Love desires an equal.
ANTHONY TROLLOPE, Duke's Children

She kissed me. I was kissed. All yielding she tossed my hair.
Kissed, she kissed me.
Me. And me now.
JAMES JOYCE, Ulysses

If you think what they call free love is fun you are mistaken.
Believe me, it's the most overrated amusement ever
invented. It has all the inconveniences of marriage
and none of its advantages.
SOMERSET MAUGHAM, Attrib.

This day by the blessing of God, my wife and I have been
married nine years – but my head being full of business,
I did not think of it, to keep it in any extraordinary manner.
But bless God for our long lives and loves and health
together, which the same God long continue, I wish from
my very heart.
SAMUEL PEPYS, *The Diary of Samuel Pepys*, 10 October 1664

Our mean lives, unsightly as they are, put on splendour and
have meaning only under the eyes of love.
VIRGINIA WOOLF, *The Waves*

'No man is offended by another man's admiration of
the woman he loves; it is the woman only
who can make it a torment.'
JANE AUSTEN, *Northanger Abbey* (Henry Tilney)

Who, being loved, is poor? Oh, no one.
OSCAR WILDE, *A Woman of No Importance*

Familiarity breeds contempt – and children.
MARK TWAIN, *Notebook*

Fond lovers' parting is sweet, painful pleasure,
Hope beaming mild on the soft parting hour;
But the dire feeling, O farewell for ever!
Anguish unmingled, and agony pure!
ROBERT BURNS, 'Thou Gloomy December'

Ordinary men take wives because possession is not possible without marriage, and ... ordinary women accept husbands because marriage is not possible without possession.
THOMAS HARDY, *Far from the Madding Crowd*

You can bear your own faults,
Why not a fault in your wife?
BENJAMIN FRANKLIN, *Poor Richard's Almanack*

To love, you have to understand the other, more than she understands herself, and to submit to her understanding of you. It is damnably difficult and painful, but it is the only thing which endures.
D. H. LAWRENCE, Letter to Sir Thomas Dunlop, 1914

'I think he's the wictim o' connubiality, as Blue Beard's domestic chaplain said, with a tear of pity, ven he buried him.'
CHARLES DICKENS, *The Pickwick Papers* (Sam Weller)

The magic of our first love is our ignorance that it will ever end.
BENJAMIN DISRAELI, *Henrietta Temple*

When a girl tells the man she likes second best about the other one – then she's in love.
F. SCOTT FITZGERALD, *The Last Tycoon*

Wine comes in at the mouth
And love comes in at the eye;
That's all we shall know for truth
Before we grow old and die.
I lift the glass to my mouth,
I look at you, and I sigh.
W. B. YEATS, 'A Drinking Song'

The Book of Life begins with a man and a woman in a garden.
It ends with Revelations.
OSCAR WILDE, *A Woman of No Importance*

I feel the sterling worth of such a young man and the
desirableness of your growing in love with him again.
I recommend this most thoroughly.
JANE AUSTEN, *Letters*, 18 November 1814

That's not life for men and women, insult and hatred.
And everybody knows that it's the very opposite
of that that is really life.
What? says Alf.
Love, says Bloom. I mean the opposite of hatred.
JAMES JOYCE, *Ulysses*

It is awful work, this love, and prevents all a man's projects of
good or glory.
LORD BYRON, Letter to Moore, 1821

Love seems the swiftest, but it is the slowest of all growths. No man or woman really knows what perfect love is until they have been married a quarter of a century.
MARK TWAIN, *Notebook*

A man should marry first, for virtue; secondly, for wit; thirdly, for beauty; and fourthly, for money.
DR JOHNSON, *Johnsonian Miscellanies*

One must learn to love, and go through a great deal of suffering to get to it, like any knight of the grail, and the journey is always *towards* the other soul, not away from it.
D. H. LAWRENCE, Letter to Sir Thomas Dunlop, 1914

'It is always incomprehensible to a man that a woman should ever refuse an offer of marriage. A man always imagines a woman to be ready for anybody who asks her.'
JANE AUSTEN, *Emma* (Emma Woodhouse)

Three things are men most liable to be cheated in:
A Horse, A Wig, A Wife.
BENJAMIN FRANKLIN, *Poor Richard's Almanack*

The natural barbarousness of man is much increased by a bachelor life.
THOMAS HARDY, *Wessex Tales*

I have often thought that every woman should marry and no man ... [But] I would not answer for myself if I could find an affectionate family with good shooting and first-rate claret.
BENJAMIN DISRAELI, *Lothair*

Excepting, always, falling off a horse there is nothing more fatally easy than marriage before the Registrar.
RUDYARD KIPLING, 'In the Pride of His Youth'

To love oneself is the beginning of a lifelong romance.
OSCAR WILDE, *An Ideal Husband*

I can't advise you [to marry me] because I think it would be beastly for you, but think how nice it would be for me. I am restless & moody & misanthropic & lazy and have no money except what I earn and if I got ill you would starve. In fact it's a lousy proposition.
EVELYN WAUGH, Letter to Laura (His Second Wife)

Love sought is good, but given unsought is better.
WILLIAM SHAKESPEARE, *Twelfth Night*

A bonie lass, I will confess,
Is pleasant to the e'e;
But without some better qualities
She's no a lass for me.
ROBERT BURNS, 'Handsome Nell'

[Marriage] resembles a pair of shears, so joined that they cannot be separated; often moving in opposite directions, yet always punishing any one who comes between them.
SYDNEY SMITH, *Memoir*

Riches are uncovering in shops: jewels, gold, and silver, flash in the goldsmith's sunny windows; and great houses cast a stately shade upon them as they pass. But through the light, and through the shade, they go on lovingly together, lost to everything around; thinking of no other riches, and no prouder home, than they have now in one another.
CHARLES DICKENS, *Dombey and Son*

Jack Sprat and his wife in the nursery rhyme, offer an ideal example of adaptation for co-existence.
ROBERT LOUIS STEVENSON, 'From His Notebook'

Keep your eyes wide open before marriage, half shut afterwards.
BENJAMIN FRANKLIN, *Poor Richard's Almanack*

Husbands and wives generally understand when opposition will be vain.
JANE AUSTEN, *Persuasion*

YOUTH AND
OLD AGE

The irritating thing about ungoverned children is that they often make as orderly and valuable men and women as do the other kind.
MARK TWAIN, *Notebook*

Solitude is surely for the young, who have time before them ... and who can, therefore, take delight in thinking.
ANTHONY TROLLOPE, *Last Chronicle of Barset*

One cannot love *lumps of flesh*, and little infants are nothing more.
DR JOHNSON, *Johnsonian Miscellanies*

Youth, which is forgiven everything, forgives itself nothing: age, which forgives itself everything, is forgiven nothing.
GEORGE BERNARD SHAW, *Maxims for Revolutionists*

'Seven years and six months!' Humpty Dumpty repeated thoughtfully. 'An uncomfortable sort of age. Now if you'd asked my advice, I'd have said "Leave off at seven" – but it's too late now.'
LEWIS CARROLL, *Through the Looking-Glass*

The greatest advance of age which I have yet found is liking a *cat* an animal I detested and becoming fond of a garden an art which I despised.
SIR WALTER SCOTT, *Letters*

Youth is wholly experimental.
ROBERT LOUIS STEVENSON, 'Letter to a Young Gentleman'

From the earliest times the old have rubbed it into the young that they are wiser than they, and before the young had discovered what nonsense this was they were old too, and it profited them to carry on the imposture.
SOMERSET MAUGHAM, Attrib.

[To Edith Evans] If a person over fifty tries too hard to be with it, they soon find they're without everything.
NOËL COWARD, Attrib.

Men become old, but they never become good.
OSCAR WILDE, Lady Windermere's Fan

One evil in old age is that as your time is come you think every little illness is the beginning of the end. When a man expects to be arrested every knock on the door is an alarm.
SYDNEY SMITH, Letter, 1836

[To a supercilious youth who said he 'simply couldn't bear fools'] 'How odd. Your mother could apparently.'
DOROTHY PARKER, Attrib.

Their elders, tired of watching the carnival with ill-concealed envy, had discovered that young liquor would take the place of young blood.
F. SCOTT FITZGERALD, 'Echoes of the Jazz Age'

———

Bliss was it in that dawn to be alive,
But to be young was very heaven!
WILLIAM WORDSWORTH, *The Prelude*

———

Neither a man nor a boy ever thinks the age he *has* is exactly the best one – he puts the *right* age a few years older or a few years younger than he is.
MARK TWAIN, *(Extract from) Captain Stormfield's Visit to Heaven*

———

[Mr Tulkinghorn] is what is called the old school –
a phrase generally meaning any school that seems
never to have been young.
CHARLES DICKENS, *Bleak House*

———

To do nothing and get something formed a
boy's idea of a manly career.
BENJAMIN DISRAELI, *Sybil*

———

A child should always say what's true
And speak when it is spoken to,
And behave mannerly at table;
At least as far as he is able.
ROBERT LOUIS STEVENSON, *A Child's Garden of Verses*

A child should not be discouraged from reading anything that he takes a liking to from a notion that it is above his reach.
DR JOHNSON, Attrib.

One does not care for girls till they are grown up.
JANE AUSTEN, *Letters*, 9 September 1814

Let thy Child's first lesson be Obedience
And the second may be what thou wilt.
BENJAMIN FRANKLIN, *Poor Richard's Almanack*

A man of eighty and upwards may be allowed to talk long because in the nature of things he cannot have long to talk.
SIR WALTER SCOTT, *The Journal of Sir Walter Scott*

A set o' dull, conceited hashes
Confuse their brains in college-classes!
They gang in stirks, and come out asses.
ROBERT BURNS, 'Epistle to J. Lapraik'

It was one of the deadliest and heaviest feelings of my life to feel that I was no longer a boy. From that moment I began to grow old in my own esteem; and in my esteem age is not estimable.
LORD BYRON, *Detached Thoughts*

All would live long, but none would be old.
BENJAMIN FRANKLIN, *Poor Richard's Almanack*

[27]

I am making a setting for my old age, a place to
influence lawless youth, with its severity and antiquity.
W. B. YEATS, Letter to John Quinn, 1918

Everybody's youth is a dream, a form of chemical madness.
F. SCOTT FITZGERALD, 'The Diamond as Big as the Ritz'

Young men, whom Aristotle thought
Unfit to hear moral philosophy.
WILLIAM SHAKESPEARE, *Troilus and Cressida*

To get back my youth I would do anything in the world,
except take exercise, get up early, or be respectable.
OSCAR WILDE, *The Picture of Dorian Gray*

I think myself that age is to a certain degree a habit.
BENJAMIN DISRAELI, *Disraeli's Reminiscences*

They [the young] talk love where we talked God. I think our
age though ossified was of the two the more sublime.
VIRGINIA WOOLF, Letter, 1 November 1928

For God's sake give me the young man who has brains enough
to make a fool of himself!
ROBERT LOUIS STEVENSON, 'Crabbed Age and Youth'

There are those who scoff at the schoolboy, calling him
frivolous and shallow. Yet it was the schoolboy who said,
'Faith is believing what you know ain't so.'
MARK TWAIN, *Following the Equator*

Invention is the talent of youth, and judgment of age; so that
our judgment grows harder to please, when we have fewer
things to offer it: this goes through the whole commerce of
life. When we are old our friends find it difficult to please us,
and are less concerned whether we be pleased or no.
JONATHAN SWIFT, *Thoughts on Various Subjects*

Real children – children who have not been spoiled by too
much notice, and thus taught to give themselves the airs of
little men and women.
LEWIS CARROLL, *The Lost Plum Cake*

Youth enters the world with very happy prejudices in
her own favour.
DR JOHNSON, *The Rambler*

Nothing in life can be more ludicrous or compatible than an
old man aping the passions of his youth.
SIR WALTER SCOTT, *The Journal of Sir Walter Scott*

O man! while in thy early years
  How prodigal of time!
Mis-spending all thy precious hours –
  Thy glorious, youthful prime!
ROBERT BURNS, 'Man was Made to Mourn'

After the sureties of youth there sets in a period of intense and intolerable complexity.

F. SCOTT FITZGERALD, *The Beautiful and Damned*

Boys between the ages of thirteen and eighteen are completely odious creatures, destructive of peace and property, uncouth, self-assertive, and generally unsuited to civilized company. Accordingly parents have to find a race of men so desperate and mercenary that they will devote their lives to keeping them away from home during the greater part of this period.

EVELYN WAUGH, *Daily Mail*, 30 August 1930

> In youth, it was a way I had
> To do my best to please,
> And change, with every passing lad,
> To suit his theories.
> But now I know the things I know,
> And do the things I do;
> And if you do not like me so,
> To hell, my love, with you!

DOROTHY PARKER, 'Indian Summer'

Every young man must be exposed to temptation: he cannot learn the ways of men without being witless to their vices. If you attempt to preserve him from danger by keeping him out of the way of it, you render him quite unfit for any style of life in which he may be placed. The great point is, not to turn him out too soon, and to give him a pilot first.

SYDNEY SMITH, *Sketches of Moral Philosophy*

There is no sadder sight than a young pessimist,
except an old optimist.
MARK TWAIN, *Notebook*

The old appear in conversation in two characters: the
critically silent and the garrulous anecdotic.
ROBERT LOUIS STEVENSON, 'Talk and Talkers'

'There is something so amiable in the prejudices of a young
mind that one is sorry to see them give way to the reception
of more general opinions.'
JANE AUSTEN, *Sense and Sensibility*, I (Colonel Brandon)

One of the pleasures of middle age is to *find out* that
one *was* right, and that one was much righter than one knew
at say seventeen or twenty-three.
EZRA POUND, *ABC of Reading*

I didn't know till 15 that there was anyone in the world
except me, and it cost me *plenty*.
F. SCOTT FITZGERALD, *The Letters*, Summer 1935

I find it poignant to look at youth in all its activity and
ardour, and most of all to watch little children playing their
merry games, and wonder what would lie before them if God
wearied of mankind.
WINSTON CHURCHILL, *Great Contemporaries*

Remember always ... that the parents buy the books, and
that the children never read them.
DR JOHNSON, *Johnsonian Miscellanies*

For youthful faults ripe virtues shall atone.
WILLIAM WORDSWORTH, 'Artegal and Elidure'

As a man grows old he wants amusement, more even than
when he is young; and then it becomes so difficult
to find amusement.
ANTHONY TROLLOPE, *Autobiography*

The greatest and wisest are flattered by the deference of youth
– so graceful and becoming in itself.
SIR WALTER SCOTT, *The Abbot*

What makes old age hard to bear is not a failing of one's
faculties, mental and physical, but the burden of one's memories.
SOMERSET MAUGHAM, Attrib.

Children may just as well play as not.
The ogre will come in any case.
JAMES JOYCE, Letter, 16 October 1925

When you've lived sixty-three years you are bound to pick
up a bit of sophistication here and there. But I was probably
sophisticated when I was five.
NOËL COWARD, Attrib.

He had reached an age where death no longer has the quality
of ghastly surprise.
F. SCOTT FITZGERALD, *The Great Gatsby*

They are always telling lies of us old fellows.
DR JOHNSON, Attrib.

Youth is a blunder; Manhood a struggle; Old Age a regret.
BENJAMIN DISRAELI, *Coningsby*

Although the ways of children cross with those of their elders
in a hundred places daily, they never go in the same direction
nor so much as lie in the same element.
ROBERT LOUIS STEVENSON, *A Child's Garden of Verses*

What a transient business is life! Very lately I was a boy; but
t'other day I was a young man; and I already begin to feel the
rigid fibre and stiffening joints of old age coming fast
o'er my frame.
ROBERT BURNS, Letter to Mrs Dunlop, 29 December 1795

It's an epitome of life – The first half of it consists of the
capacity to enjoy without the chance; the last half consists of
the chance without the capacity.
MARK TWAIN, *Letters*

I am fond of children (except boys).
LEWIS CARROLL, *Life and Letters*

The young can't believe in the youth of their fathers.
F. Scott Fitzgerald, *The Letters*, 7 July 1938

People ought to be one of two things, young or old. No –
what's the use of fooling? People ought to be
one of two things, young or dead.
Dorothy Parker, Attrib.

From the mind of childhood there is more history and more
philosophy to be fished up than from all the printed volumes
in a library.
Robert Louis Stevenson, 'Rosa Quo Locorum'

You think it horrible that lust and rage
Should dance attention upon my old age;
They were not such a plague when I was young;
What else have I to spur me into song?
W. B. Yeats, 'The Spur'

The old believe everything: the middle-aged suspect
everything: the young know everything.
Oscar Wilde, *Phrases and Philosophies for the Use of the Young*

Many a clever boy is flogged into a dunce and many an
original composition corrected into mediocrity.
Sir Walter Scott, *Journal*

One grows more carnal and more mortal as one grows older.
Only youth has a taste of immortality.
D. H. LAWRENCE, *Lady Chatterley's Lover*

If a man would register all his opinions upon love, politics,
religion, learning, etc., beginning from his youth, and so
go on to old age, what a bundle of inconsistencies would
appear at last?
JONATHAN SWIFT, *Thoughts on Various Subjects*

It's all the young can do for the old,
to shock them and keep them up to date.
GEORGE BERNARD SHAW, *Fanny's First Play*

Seventy is old enough. After that there is too much risk.
MARK TWAIN, *Following the Equator*

Children are entertained with stories full of prodigies; their
experience not being sufficient to cause them to be so readily
startled at deviations from the natural course of life.
DR JOHNSON, Attrib.

Nature and Animals

'I have just learned to love a hyacinth.'
JANE AUSTEN, *Northanger Abbey* (Catherine Morland)

When Nature her great masterpiece designed,
And framed her last, best work, the human mind,
Her eye intent on all the wondrous plan,
She formed of various stuff the various Man.
ROBERT BURNS, 'To Robert Graham'

One touch of nature makes the whole world kin.
WILLIAM SHAKESPEARE, *Troilus and Cressida*

Odd things animals. All dogs look up to you. All cats look
down to you. Only a pig looks at you as an equal.
WINSTON CHURCHILL, Attrib.

'In most gardens', the Tiger-lily said, 'they make the beds too
soft – so that the flowers are always asleep.'
LEWIS CARROLL, *Through the Looking Glass*

Here he is, wandering alone, waiting duteously on Nature,
while she unfolds a page of stern, of silent, and of solemn
poetry beneath his attentive gaze.
CHARLOTTE BRONTË, *Shirley*

God was palpably present in the country, and the devil had
gone with the world to town.
THOMAS HARDY, *Far From the Madding Crowd*

A man who will plant a poplar, a willow, or even a blue-gum in a treeless country – how good is he! But the man who will plant an oak will surely feel the greenness of its foliage and the pleasantness of its shade when he is lying down, down beneath the sod!
ANTHONY TROLLOPE 'Western Province'

It seems to me that we all look at Nature too much, and live with her too little.
OSCAR WILDE, *De Profundis*

The summer and the country have no charms for me. I look forward anxiously to the return of bad weather, coal fires, and good society in a crowded city. I have no relish for the country; it is a kind of healthy grave. I am afraid you are not exempt from the delusion of flowers, green turf, and birds; they all afford slight gratification, but not worth an hour of rational conversation: a rational conversation in sufficient quantities is only to be had from the congregation of a million people in one spot.
SYDNEY SMITH, Letter, 1838

I always knew that the line of Nature is crooked, that, though we dig the canal-beds as straight as we can, the rivers run hither and thither in their wildness.
W. B. YEATS, 'What is Popular Poetry?'

Humanity always fails me: Nature never.
GEORGE BERNARD SHAW, *Too True To Be Good*

It is true that a writer should hold a mirror up to nature, although there are certain aspects of nature which would be better unreflected.
NoËL COWARD, *Sunday Times*, 1961

[To a friend who was upset that he had to get rid of his cat]
'Have you tried curiosity?'
DOROTHY PARKER, Attrib.

In the climate of England there are, for the lover of Nature, days which are worth months ... even years.
WILLIAM WORDSWORTH, *Guide to the Lakes*

It is a very inconvenient habit of kittens ... that, whatever you say to them, they *always* purr ... How can you talk with a person if they *always* say the same thing?
LEWIS CARROLL, *Alice in Wonderland*

As long as I retain my feeling and my passion for Nature, I can partly soften or subdue my other passions and resist or endure those of others.
LORD BYRON, Letter to Isaac d'Israeli, 1822

Let others love the city,
And gaudy show, at sunny noon;
Gie me the lonely valley,
The dewy eve, the rising moon.
ROBERT BURNS, 'Sae Flaxen were her Ringlets'

Air and cleanliness are the two most important things
in this life.
D. H. LAWRENCE, Letter to Cynthia Asquith, 1913

Jock, when ye hae naething else to do, ye may be ay sticking
in a tree; it will be growing, Jock, when ye're sleeping.
SIR WALTER SCOTT, Heart of Mid-Lothian

A swarm of bees is simply a single animal whose many limbs
are not quite close together.
LEWIS CARROLL, Sylvie and Bruno Concluded

We have reached a degree of intelligence which Nature never
contemplated when framing her laws, and for which she
consequently has provided no adequate satisfactions.
THOMAS HARDY, Tess of the d'Urbervilles

Nature who has played so many queer tricks upon us, making
us so unequally of clay and diamonds, of rainbow and granite,
and stuffed them into a case of the most incongruous ...
VIRGINIA WOOLF, Orlando

A forest is like the ocean, monotonous only to the ignorant. It
is a life of ceaseless variety.
BENJAMIN DISRAELI, Disraeli's Reminiscences

At the office in the morning and did business. By and By we
are called to Sir W. Batten to see the strange creature that
Capt. Holmes hath brought with him from Guiny; it is a great
baboone, but so much like a man in most things, that (though
they say there is a species of them) yet I cannot believe but
that it is a monster got of a man and a she-baboone. I do
believe it already understands much English; and I am of the
mind it might be taught to speak or make signs.
SAMUEL PEPYS, *The Diary of Samuel Pepys*, 24 August 1661

In Nature's infinite book of secrecy
A little can I read.
WILLIAM SHAKESPEARE, *Antony and Cleopatra*

To me the meanest flower that blows can give
Thoughts that do often lie too deep for tears.
WILLIAM WORDSWORTH, 'Ode: Intimations of Immortality'

Give me English birds and English trees, English dogs and
Irish horses, English rivers and English ships; but English
men! No, No, No!
GEORGE BERNARD SHAW, *In Good King Charles's Golden Days*

'I have seen such storms in hilly districts in Yorkshire; and at
their riotous climax, while the sky was all cataract, the earth
all flood, I have remembered the Deluge.'
CHARLOTTE BRONTË, *Shirley* (Shirley Keeldar)

The voice of Nature loudly cries,
And many a message from the skies,
That something in us never dies.
ROBERT BURNS, 'New Year's Day'

—

All I say is, nobody has any business to go around looking like
a horse and behaving as if it were all right. You don't catch
horses going around looking like people, do you?
DOROTHY PARKER, 'Horsie

—

After reading Thoreau I felt how much I have lost by
leaving nature out of my life.
F. SCOTT FITZGERALD, *The Letters*, 11 March 1939

—

I wonder if the snow loves the trees and fields, that it kisses
them so gently?
LEWIS CARROLL, *Through the Looking-Glass*

—

'Oh!' cried Marianne, 'with what transporting sensations have
I formerly seen them fall! How have I delighted as I walked,
to see them driven in showers about me by the wind! What
feelings have they, the season, the air altogether inspired!
Now there is no one to regard them. They are seen only as
a nuisance swept hastily off, and driven as much as possible
from the sight.'
'It is not everyone,' said Elinor, 'who has your passion for
dead leaves.'
JANE AUSTEN, *Sense and Sensibility*, I (Marianne and Elinor Dashwood)

[43]

Perception and Morality

'Let us be moral. Let us contemplate existence.'
CHARLES DICKENS, *Martin Chuzzlewit* (Seth Pecksniff)

You can't learn too soon that the most useful thing about a principle is that it can always be sacrificed to expediency.
SOMERSET MAUGHAM, Attrib.

They say best men are moulded out of faults,
And, for the most become much more the better
For being a little bad.
WILLIAM SHAKESPEARE, *Measure for Measure*

There is nothing in this world constant, but inconstancy.
JONATHAN SWIFT, 'A Tritical Essay upon the Faculties of the Mind'

Whatever your sins are I hope you never get to justify them to yourself.
F. SCOTT FITZGERALD, *The Letters*, 5 July 1937

Tragedy is lack of experience.
D. H. LAWRENCE, *Sun*

Shut your eyes hard against the recollection of your sins. Do not be afraid, you will not be able to forget them.
ROBERT LOUIS STEVENSON, 'Reflections and Remarks on Human Life'

All that I have said and done,
Now that I am old and ill,
Turns into a question till
I lie awake night after night
And never get the answer right.
Did that play of mine send out
Certain men the English shot?
Did my words put too great strain
On that woman's reeling brain?
Could my spoken words have checked
That whereby a house lay wrecked?
W. B. YEATS, 'Man and the Echo'

'I have meant to do right; but, Janet, it is so hard to do right.'
ANTHONY TROLLOPE, *Vicar of Bullhampton* (Mary Lowther)

Sin is not hurtful because it is forbidden. But it is forbidden
because it is hurtful.
BENJAMIN FRANKLIN, *Poor Richard's Almanack*

There is such a thing as loyalty to a man's own better self;
and from those who have not that, God help me, how am I to
look for loyalty to others.
ROBERT LOUIS STEVENSON, 'Lay Morals'

They that have power to hurt and will do none,
That do not do the thing they most do show,
Who, moving others, are themselves as stone,
Unmoved, cold and to temptation slow ...
They are the lords and owners of their faces ...
WILLIAM SHAKESPEARE, Sonnet 94

Though I think it useful and creditable to attack what ought
to be attacked, and expedient to use such weapons in attack
as God has given us – gravity or gaiety, sense or sarcasm – yet
there is moderation to be used in the frequency of attacks,
and in the bitterness of attacks: and in both these points
I believe I have sinned.
SYDNEY SMITH, Letter, 1824

To act rightly simply because it is one's duty is proper; but a
good action which is the result of no law of reflection shines
more than any.
THOMAS HARDY, *Desperate Remedies*

It is absurd to divide people into good and bad. People are
either charming or tedious.
OSCAR WILDE, *Lady Windermere's Fan*

There is a Moral Sense, and there is an Immoral Sense. History
shows us that the Moral Sense enables us to perceive morality
and how to avoid it, and that the Immoral Sense enables us to
perceive immorality and how to enjoy it.
MARK TWAIN, *Following the Equator*

It is so tiresome of our little sins to look foolish when they are found out, instead of wicked.

SOMERSET MAUGHAM, Attrib.

O wad some Power the giftie gie us
To see oursels as ithers see us!

ROBERT BURNS, 'To a Louse'

It's discouraging to think how many people are shocked by honesty and how few by deceit.

NOËL COWARD, *Blithe Spirit*

The cruellest lies are often told in silence.

ROBERT LOUIS STEVENSON, 'The Truth of Intercourse'

It is better to be narrow minded than to have no mind, to hold limited and rigid principles than none at all. That is the danger which faces so many people today – to have no considered opinions on any subject, to put up with what is wasteful and harmful with the excuse that 'there is good in everything'.

EVELYN WAUGH, *Essays*

I don't believe in morality. I'm a disciple of Bernard Shaw.

GEORGE BERNARD SHAW, *The Doctor's Dilemma*

She has a world of ready wealth,
Our minds and hearts to bless –
Spontaneous wisdom breathed by health,
Truth breathed by cheerfulness.
WILLIAM WORDSWORTH, 'The Tables Turned'

In the sun men are objective, in the mist and snow,
subjective. Subjectivity is largely a question of the thickness
of your overcoat.
D. H. LAWRENCE, 'Giovanni Verga'

My heart laments that
Virtue cannot live
Out of the teeth of emulation [envy].
WILLIAM SHAKESPEARE, *Julius Caesar*

How cheerfully he seems to grin,
And how neatly spreads his claws.
And welcomes little fishes in
With gently smiling jaws.
LEWIS CARROLL, *Alice in Wonderland*

Out of chaos God made a world, and out of
high passions comes a people.
LORD BYRON, *Diary*, 1821

The secret, shameful things are most terribly beautiful.
D. H. LAWRENCE, *The Rainbow*

The thoughts of worldly men are for ever regulated by a moral law of gravitation, which, like the physical one, holds them down to earth.

CHARLES DICKENS, *Barnaby Rudge*

Men moralise among ruins.

BENJAMIN DISRAELI, *Tancred*

The only true way to make the mass of mankind see the beauty of justice is by showing them in pretty plain terms the consequences of injustice.

SYDNEY SMITH, *Peter Plymley's Letters*

Gentleness and cheerfulness, these come before all morality; they are the perfect duties.

ROBERT LOUIS STEVENSON, 'A Christmas Sermon'

Morals are an acquirement – like music, like a foreign language, like piety, poetry, paralysis – no man is born with them. I wasn't myself, I started poor. I hadn't a single moral. There is hardly a man in this house that is poorer than I was then.

MARK TWAIN, *Speeches*, 1923

I can resist everything except temptation.

OSCAR WILDE, *Lady Windermere's Fan*

The Light of Lights
Looks always on the motive, not the deed,
The Shadow of Shadows on the deed alone.
W. B. YEATS, *The Countess Cathleen*

Every man to himself is the centre of the whole world;
the axle on which it all turns. All knowledge is but his own
perception of the things around him.
ANTHONY TROLLOPE, *Can You Forgive Her?*

If we do not run some hazard in our attempts to do good
where is the merit of them?
SIR WALTER SCOTT, *The Journal of Sir Walter Scott*

Vision is the art of seeing things invisible.
JONATHAN SWIFT, *Thoughts on Various Subjects*

Man's inhumanity to man
Makes countless thousands mourn!
ROBERT BURNS, 'Man was Made to Mourn'

See how yon justice rails upon yon simple thief ...
Change places and, handy-dandy,
which is the justice, which is the thief?
WILLIAM SHAKESPEARE, *King Lear*

Morality consists in suspecting other people of not being
legally married.
GEORGE BERNARD SHAW, *The Doctor's Dilemma*

> True dignity abides with him alone
> Who, in the silent hour of inward thought,
> Can still suspect, and still revere himself,
> In lowliness of heart.
> WILLIAM WORDSWORTH, 'Lines'

Beauty is a mystery. You can neither eat it nor make flannel
out of it.
D. H. LAWRENCE, 'Sex versus Loveliness'

There is such a thing as loyalty to a man's own better self;
and from those who have not that, God help me, how am I to
look for loyalty to others.
ROBERT LOUIS STEVENSON, 'Lay Morals'

> Of course I am a moralist, not in the conventional sense,
> but I am always preaching.
> NOËL COWARD, New York press, 1929

Cruelty is the law pervading all nature and society.
THOMAS HARDY, Attrib.

A man should not be without morals; it is better to have bad
morals than none at all.
MARK TWAIN, *Notebook*

Some rise by sin, and some by virtue fall.
WILLIAM SHAKESPEARE, *Measure for Measure*

There is no such thing as abstract morality.
SOMERSET MAUGHAM, Attrib.

They say 'Virtue is its own reward', – it certainly should be
paid well for its trouble.
LORD BYRON, *Journal*, 1813

The basis for every scandal is an immoral certainty.
OSCAR WILDE, *The Picture of Dorian Gray*

To every view of morals there are two sides: what is demanded
by man; what is exacted by the conditions of life.
ROBERT LOUIS STEVENSON, 'Lay Morals'

The blood also thinks, inside a man, darkly and ponderously.
It thinks in desires and revulsions, and it makes strange
conclusions ... My blood tells me there is no such thing
as perfection. There is the long endless venture into
consciousness down an ever-dangerous valley of days.
D. H. LAWRENCE, 'BOOKS'

Satire is a sort of glass, wherein beholders do generally
discover everybody's face but their own.

JONATHAN SWIFT, *The Battle of the Books*

—

O what a tangled web we weave,
When first we practise to deceive!

SIR WALTER SCOTT, *Marmion*

—

If the desire to kill and the opportunity to kill came always
together, who would escape hanging?

MARK TWAIN, *Following the Equator*

—

The passing moment's all we rest on!

ROBERT BURNS, 'Sketch – New Year's Day'

POLITICS
AND WAR

There is no act of treachery or meanness of which a political party is not capable; for in politics there is no honour.
BENJAMIN DISRAELI, *Vivian Grey*

Most of the world's troubles seem to come from people who are too busy. If only politicians and scientists were lazier, how much happier we should all be.
EVELYN WAUGH, *Essays*

I used to be fond of war when I was a younger man, and longed heartily to be a soldier; but now I think there is no prayer in the service with which I could close more earnestly, than 'Send peace in our time, good Lord'.
SIR WALTER SCOTT, *Letters*

Some men change their Party for the sake of their principles; others change their principles for the sake of their Party.
WINSTON CHURCHILL, General Election Speech, 1906

The pity is that politics are looked on as being a game for politicians, just as cricket is a game for cricketers; not as the serious duties of political trustees.
THOMAS HARDY, *The Well-Beloved*

If I could see good measures pursued, I care not a farthing who is in power, but I have a passionate love for common justice, and for common sense, and I abhor and despise every man who builds up his political fortune upon their ruin.
SYDNEY SMITH, *Peter Plymley's Letters*

Last night we had a meeting, to discuss politics here.
The villagers all sat silent. The middle classes talked.
VIRGINIA WOOLF, Letter, 5 October 1938

Sir, that is all visionary. I would not give half a guinea to live
under one form of government rather than another. It is of no
moment to the happiness of an individual.
DR JOHNSON, Attrib.

The only way a nation can render itself safe is by
civilising its neighbours.
EZRA POUND, *Selected Prose*

Politics are, indeed, the forge in which nations are made, and
the smith has been so long busy making Ireland according to
His will that she may well have some important destiny.
W. B. YEATS, 'The Literary Movement in Ireland'

Never in the field of human conflict was so much
owed by so many to so few.
WINSTON CHURCHILL, Speech to the House of Commons,
20 August 1940

The heavens themselves, the planets, and this centre
Observe degree, priority, and place,
Insisture, course, proportion, season, form,
Office and custom, all in line of order.
WILLIAM SHAKESPEARE, *Troilus and Cressida*

'What is peace? Is it war? No. Is it strife? No.
Is it lovely, and gentle, and beautiful, and pleasant,
and serene, and joyful? O yes!'
CHARLES DICKENS, *Bleak House* (Mr Chadband)

There is nothing more tyrannical than a strong popular
feeling among a democratic people.
ANTHONY TROLLOPE, *North America*

Politics is perhaps the only profession for which no
preparation is thought necessary.
ROBERT LOUIS STEVENSON, 'Yoshida-Torajiro'

We are all conservatives but what exactly are we trying to
conserve? Looking over our shoulders from the ramparts do
we see the unconquered citadel already in decay?
EVELYN WAUGH, *Essays*

'I had no idea that the law had been so great a slavery.'
JANE AUSTEN, *Emma* (Mr Elton)

Only people who look dull ever get into the House of
Commons, and only people who are dull ever succeed there.
OSCAR WILDE, *An Ideal Husband*

The defects of a class are more perceptible to the class
immediately below it than to itself.

THOMAS HARDY, *Life*

I always shrink from any expression of
political sentimentalism.

BENJAMIN DISRAELI, Attrib.

Our conduct to Ireland, during the whole of this war, has been
that of a man who subscribes to hospitals, weeps at charity
sermons, carries out broth and blankets to beggars, and then
comes home and beats his wife and children.

SYDNEY SMITH, *Peter Plymley's Letters*

It has been said that Democracy is the worst form of
government except all those other forms that have
been tried from time to time.

WINSTON CHURCHILL, Speech in the House of Commons,
11 November 1947

Hitlers are bred by slaves.

VIRGINIA WOOLF, 'Thoughts on Peace in an Air Raid'

That mighty mystery the world does so grope after in open
day, that shews nothing to me more obvious than
(not only the certainty) but inevitableness of a war. But if
faith be only the evidence of things not seen, infidelity must
be a non-discerning of things visible.

SAMUEL PEPYS, *Further Correspondence of Samuel Pepys*

Your deepest pools, like your deepest politicians and philosophers, often turn out more shallow than expected.
SIR WALTER SCOTT, *The Journal of Sir Walter Scott*

There is no freedom in Europe – that's certain; it is besides a worn-out portion of the globe.
LORD BYRON, Letter to Hobhouse, 1819

I am of that odious class of men called democrats, and of that class I shall for ever continue.
WILLIAM WORDSWORTH, *Letters*

The reasonable man adapts himself to the world: the unreasonable one persists in trying to adapt the world to himself. Therefore all progress depends on the unreasonable man.
GEORGE BERNARD SHAW, *Man and Superman*

No Government can be long secure without a formidable Opposition.
BENJAMIN DISRAELI, *Coningsby*

The only foundation of political liberty is the spirit of the people: and the only circumstance which makes a lively impression upon their senses, and powerfully reminds them of their importance, their power, and their rights, is the periodical choice of their representatives.
SYDNEY SMITH, *Edinburgh Review*, 1803

Nothing effectual will be accomplished in the cause of *Peace* till the sentiment of *Patriotism* be freed from the narrow meaning attached to it in the past ... and be extended to the whole globe.

THOMAS HARDY, *Life*

A private, ironically called a 'free' press, of the kind which flourishes in France, England and the United States – where no responsibility curbs its extravagances, where the news is merely a bait to attract attention to the advertisements – is the worst possible guide to popular sympathies.

EVELYN WAUGH, *Essays*

If we would learn what the human race really is at bottom, we need only observe it at election times

MARK TWAIN, *Autobiography*

Perhaps there is nothing so dangerous to a modern state, when politics takes the place of theology, as a bunch of martyrs. A bunch of martyrs (1916) were the bomb and we are living in the explosion.

W. B. YEATS, Letter to Olivia Shakespeare, 9 October 1922

My political faith can be expressed in a word: Monarchies, constitutional or unconstitutional, disgust me. Kings are mountebanks.

JAMES JOYCE, Attrib.

Wars are made in order to create debts ... War is the highest
form of sabotage, the most atrocious form of sabotage.
EZRA POUND, *Selected Prose*

No, I have no social causes. I can't think of any offhand.
If I did, they'd be very offhand.
NOËL COWARD, *Sunday Times,* 1969

The inherent vice of Capitalism is the unequal sharing of
blessings; the inherent virtue of Socialism
is the equal sharing of miseries.
WINSTON CHURCHILL, Speech to the House of Commons,
22 October 1945

Patriotism is the last refuge of a scoundrel.
DR JOHNSON, Attrib.

I am not a member of any political party. The only group I
have ever been affiliated with is that not especially brave
little band that hid its nakedness of heart and mind under the
out-of-date garment of a sense of humor. I heard someone say,
and so I said it too, that ridicule is the most effective weapon.
I don't suppose I ever really believed it, but it was easy and
comforting, and so I said it. Well, now I know. I know that
there are things that never have been funny, and never will
be. And I know that ridicule may be a shield,
but it is not a weapon.
DOROTHY PARKER, Attrib.

I now consider the war between France and England no longer
as an occasional quarrel or temporary dispute, but as an
antipathy and national horror, after the same kind as subsists
between the kite and the crow, or the churchwarden and the
pauper, the weasel and the rat, the parson and the Deist,
the bailiff and the half-pay Captain, etc., who have
persecuted each other from the beginning of time, and will
peak, swear, fly, preach at, and lie in wait for each other
till the end of time.
SYDNEY SMITH, *Memoir*

Get thee glass eyes,
And, like a scurvy politician, seem
To see the thing thou dost not.
WILLIAM SHAKESPEARE, *King Lear*

My puzzle is, ought artists now to become politicians? My
instinct says no; but I'm not sure that I can justify my instinct.
VIRGINIA WOOLF, Letter, 24 August 1940

Conservatism is not estimable in itself, nor is Change, or
Radicalism. To conserve the existing good, to supplant the
existing bad by good, is to act on a true political principle,
which is neither Conservative or Radical.
THOMAS HARDY, *Life*

The House of Commons will never ascertain their privileges
nor be bound by their orders; and yet expect the King should.
SAMUEL PEPYS, *Samuel Pepys's Naval Minutes*

It is part of Mr Chapman's thesis that no one gains anything
in war. This of course is true, absolutely. War is an absolute
loss, but it admits of degrees; it is very bad to fight,
but it is worse to lose.
EVELYN WAUGH, *Essays*

The deities that I adore
Are social Peace and Plenty;
I'm better pleased to make one more,
Than by the death of twenty.
ROBERT BURNS, 'I Murder Hate'

Parliament can compel people to obey or to submit,
but it cannot compel them to agree.
WINSTON CHURCHILL, Speech to the House of Commons,
27 September 1926

One individual always manages his own concerns
better than those of the country can be managed.
SIR WALTER SCOTT, *Letters*

Parliament seems to me the very place which a man of action
should avoid ... in this age it is not Parliament which does
the real work.
BENJAMIN DISRAELI, *Tancred*

The two maxims of any great man at court are,
always to keep his countenance, and never to keep his word.
JONATHAN SWIFT, *Thoughts on Various Subjects*

Democracies have fallen, they have always fallen,
because humanity craves the outstanding personality.
And hitherto no democracy has provided sufficient place
for such an individuality.
EZRA POUND, *Literary Essays*

In rivers and bad Governments,
The lightest things swim at the top.
BENJAMIN FRANKLIN, *Poor Richard's Almanack*

To create man was a fine and original idea; but to add the
sheep was tautology.
MARK TWAIN, *Notebook*

Between my politics and my mysticism I shall hardly
have my head turned with popularity.
W. B. YEATS, Letter to Lady Gregory, 1901

It is quite useless to declare that all men are born free if you
deny that they are born good. Guarantee a man's goodness
and his liberty will take care of itself.
GEORGE BERNARD SHAW, *Major Barbara*

The distinctions of Left and Right are now becoming as
meaningless and mischievous as the circus colours of
the Byzantine Empire.
EVELYN WAUGH, *Essays*

Political virtues are developed at the expense of moral ones.
WILLIAM WORDSWORTH, Letter to the Bishop of Landaff

The story of the human race is War. Except for brief and
precarious interludes, there has never been peace in the world.
WINSTON CHURCHILL, *The World Crisis*

Where gentry, title, wisdom
Cannot conclude but by the Yea and No
Of general ignorance, it must omit
Real necessities ...
Purpose so barred, it follows
Nothing is done to purpose.
WILLIAM SHAKESPEARE, *Coriolanus*

It is very unfair to expect a politician to live in private
up to the statements he makes in public.
SOMERSET MAUGHAM, Attrib.

We are all agreed as to our own liberty; we would have as
much of it as we can get; but we are not agreed as to the
liberty of others; for in proportion as we take, others must lose.
DR JOHNSON, Attrib.

War is a huge entrainement.
ROBERT LOUIS STEVENSON, *With Stevenson in Samoa*

I was all for war. Now I am all for peace.
WINSTON CHURCHILL, Attrib.

> I am sufficiently behind the scenes to know the worth of
> political life. I am quite an Infidel about it,
> and shall never be converted.
> CHARLES DICKENS, *David Copperfield*

As long as war is regarded as wicked, it will always have its
fascination. When it is looked upon as vulgar,
it will cease to be popular.
OSCAR WILDE, *The Critic as Artist*

I admit the immense difficulty of encountering any argument
that is based on 'unconstitutional' objections. I never yet have
found any definition of what that epithet means, and I believe
that, with the single exception of the word 'un-English', it
baffles discussion more than any other in our language.
BENJAMIN DISRAELI, Speech to the House of Commons, 26 April 1858

> Politics – what are they? Just another, extra large, commercial
> wrangle over buying and selling – nothing else.
> D. H. LAWRENCE, 'Democracy'

In politics if thou would'st mix
And mean thy fortunes be,
Bear this in mind: Be deaf and blind,
Let great folks hear and see.
ROBERT BURNS, 'Politics'

In war, it is notorious, opponents soon forget the cause of their quarrel, continue the fight for the sake of fighting and in the process assume a resemblance to what they abhorred.
EVELYN WAUGH, *Essays*

War, disguise it as you may, is but a dirty, shoddy business, which only a fool would play at.
WINSTON CHURCHILL, *The Caged Lion*

I'm not particularly interested in reforming the human race. Indeed, if I did there would be nothing to write about.
NOËL COWARD, Attrib.

I fear the representatives of the collective opinion.
W. B. YEATS, *Memoirs*, December 1908

The subject of foreign news and the political and military situation of the country are themes upon which every man thinks himself qualified to have an opinion.
SIR WALTER SCOTT, *Antiquary*

Change is inevitable.
In a progressive country change is constant.
BENJAMIN DISRAELI, Speech in Edinburgh, 29 October 1867

There is of a truth nothing manly or sterling in any part of the Government.
JOHN KEATS, Letter to George and Georgiana Keats, October 1818

That awful power, the public opinion of a nation, is created in
America by a horde of ignorant, self-complacent simpletons
who failed at ditching and shoemaking and fetched up in
journalism on their way to the poorhouse.
MARK TWAIN, *Speeches*, 1923

I should think that I had lived to little purpose if my notions
on the subject of Government
had undergone no modification.
WILLIAM WORDSWORTH, *Letters*

The first mistake in public business is the going into it.
BENJAMIN FRANKLIN, *Poor Richard's Almanack*

Revolutions come from the top.
They are produced by rottenness at the top.
EZRA POUND, *Poetry and Prose Contributions to Journals*

All government without the consent of the governed
is the very definition of slavery.
JONATHAN SWIFT, *Drapier's Letters*

In wartime ... truth is so precious that she should always
be attended by a bodyguard of lies.
WINSTON CHURCHILL, *The Second World War*, V

It has been observed that they who most loudly clamour for liberty do not most liberally grant it.

Dr Johnson, *The Lives of the Poets*

[Reply to Bulwer Lytton]
Damn your principles! Stick to your party.

Benjamin Disraeli, Attrib.

Kenneth Tynan ... is deeply scared of the atomic bomb. I mean genuinely, gibberingly scared! This I find surprising. It seems to me far too vast a nightmare to be frightened of.

Noël Coward, *The Noël Coward Diaries*, 12 January 1963

Ambition – the soldier's virtue.

William Shakespeare, *Antony and Cleopatra*

I would never belong to any club, or trades union, and God's the same to my mind.

D. H. Lawrence, *St Mawr*

My faith in the people governing is, on the whole, infinitesimal; my faith in the people governed is, on the whole, illimitable.

Charles Dickens, Speech, 27 September 1869

There will be no permanent peace in Europe till Bonaparte sleeps with the tyrants of old.

Sir Walter Scott, *Letters*

Coldly they went about to raise
To life and make more dread
Abominations of old days,
That men believed were dead.

They paid the price to reach their goal
Across a world in flame;
But their own hate slew their own soul
Before that victory came.
RUDYARD KIPLING, 'The Outlaws'

The radical of one century is the conservative of the next.
The radical invents the views.
When he has worn them out the conservative adopts them.
MARK TWAIN, Notebook

Every man, as a member of the commonwealth, ought to be
content with the possession of his own opinion in private,
without perplexing his neighbour or disturbing the public.
JONATHAN SWIFT, Thoughts on Religion

A man who entertains in his mind any political doctrine,
except as a means of improving the condition of his fellows,
I regard as a political intriguer, a charlatan, and a conjuror.
ANTHONY TROLLOPE, Autobiography

Battles are won by slaughter and manoeuvre. The greater the
general, the more he contributes in manoeuvre,
the less he demands in slaughter.
WINSTON CHURCHILL, The World Crisis

[73]

Progress to what and from where ... The European talks
of progress because by an ingenious application of some
scientific acquirements he has established a society which has
mistaken comfort for civilization.
BENJAMIN DISRAELI, *Tancred*

'Wotever is, is right, as the young nobleman sveetly remarked
ven they put him down in the pension list `cos his mother's
uncle's vife's grandfather vunce lit the king's pipe vith a
portable tinder-box.'
CHARLES DICKENS, *The Pickwick Papers* (Sam Weller)

A Conservative Government is an organised hypocrisy.
BENJAMIN DISRAELI, Speech to the House of Commons, 17 March 1845

Hurrah for revolution and more cannon-shot!
A beggar upon horseback lashes a beggar on foot.
Hurrah for revolution and cannon come again!
The beggars have changed places, but the lash goes on.
W. B. YEATS, 'The Great Day'

The Lords have passed the Suffrage Bill. I don't feel much
more important – perhaps slightly so.
VIRGINIA WOOLF, *Diary*, 11 January 1918

Populations should not be taught to gain public ends by
private crime ...
ROBERT LOUIS STEVENSON, Letter to Mrs Jenkin, April 1887

The world never yet saw so extravagant a government as the
Government of England. Not only is economy not practised –
but it is despised … Such a scene of extravagance,
corruption, and expense as must paralyse the industry, and
mar the fortunes, of the most industrious, spirited people that
ever existed.
Sydney Smith, *Edinburgh Review*, 1827

First mind you steer clear o' the grog-sellers' huts,
For they sell you Fixed Bay'nets that rots out your guts –
Ay, drink that 'ud eat the live steel from your butts –
An' it's bad for the young British soldier …

When first under fire an' you're wishful to duck
Don't look nor take 'eed at teh man that is struck.
Be thankful you're livin' an' trust to your luck
And march to your front like a soldier …

If your officer's dead and the sergeants look white,
Remember it's ruin to run from a fight:
So take open order, lie down, and sit tight,
And wait for supports like a soldier …

When you're wounded and left on Afghanistan's plains,
And the women come out to cut up what remains,
Jest roll to your rifle and blow out your brains
An' go to your Gawd like a soldier.
Rudyard Kipling, 'The Young British Soldier'

We live under a regime which makes it an avowed purpose ... to produce the modern two-class state of officials and proletariat.
EVELYN WAUGH, *Essays*

For God's sake don't talk politics. I'm not interested in politics. The only thing that interests me is style.
JAMES JOYCE, Attrib.

Victory, victory at all costs, victory in spite of all terror, victory however long and hard the road might be; for without victory there is no survival.
WINSTON CHURCHILL, Speech to the House of Commons, 13 May 1940

A pretty air in an opera is prettier there than it could be anywhere else, I suppose, just as an honest man in politics shines more than he would elsewhere.
MARK TWAIN, *Tramp*

Democracy simply means the bludgeoning of the people by the people for the people.
OSCAR WILDE, *The Soul of Man under Socialism*

Happiness and Pleasure

We should learn to take our pleasures *quickly* and
our pains *slowly*.
LEWIS CARROLL, *Sylvie and Bruno*

Pleasure is the only thing worth having a theory about.
OSCAR WILDE, *The Picture of Dorian Gray*

Sometimes it is harder to deprive oneself of a
pain than of a pleasure.
F. SCOTT FITZGERALD, *Tender is the Night*

Good friends, good books and a sleepy conscience:
this is the ideal life.
MARK TWAIN, *Notebook*

I suppose we are meant to be happy, but I don't believe the
best way of being that is to try upset other people's happiness.
SOMERSET MAUGHAM, Attrib.

In short, if it be my lot to crawl, I will crawl contentedly;
if to fly, I will fly with alacrity; but as long
as I can possibly avoid it I will never be unhappy.
SYDNEY SMITH, Letter, 1809

Happiness is but a name,
Make Content and Ease thy aim.
ROBERT BURNS, 'Written in Friars' Carse Hermitage'

We ought to feel a deep cheerfulness, as I may say, that a
happy Providence kept it from being any worse.
THOMAS HARDY, *Far from the Madding Crowd*

God forgive me, I do still see that my nature is not quite
conquered, but will esteem pleasure above all things; though,
yet in the middle of it, it hath reluctancy after my business,
which is neglected by my following my pleasure.
However, music and women I cannot but give way to,
whatever my business is.
SAMUEL PEPYS, *The Diary of Samuel Pepys*, 9 March 1666

There is no duty we so much underrate as the duty
of being happy.
ROBERT LOUIS STEVENSON, 'An Apology for Idlers'

Brevity is the soul of wit.
WILLIAM SHAKESPEARE, *Hamlet*

There is no happiness in this life but in intellect and virtue.
WILLIAM WORDSWORTH, *Letters*

A lifetime of happiness!
No man could bear it: it would be hell on earth.
GEORGE BERNARD SHAW, *Man and Superman*

Nothing is more hopeless than a scheme of merriment.
DR JOHNSON, *The Idler*

'One half of the world cannot understand the
pleasures of the other.'
JANE AUSTEN, *Emma* (Emma Woodhouse)

Happiness was but the occasional episode
in a general drama of pain.
THOMAS HARDY, *The Mayor of Casterbridge*

When we are happy we are always good, but when we are
good we are not always happy.
OSCAR WILDE, *The Picture of Dorian Gray*

Excitement is a great step towards happiness particularly to
those who are over sixty.
ANTHONY TROLLOPE, *Blackwoods*

Go into the sunshine and be happy with what you see.
WINSTON CHURCHILL, *Thoughts and Adventures*

There is a goal, but the goal is neither love nor death. It is
a goal neither infinite nor eternal. It is the realm of calm
delight, it is the other-kingdom of bliss.
D. H. LAWRENCE, 'Love'

I believe wholeheartedly in pleasure. I am very light-minded
and extremely serious.
Noël Coward, *Daily Mail*, 1962

'People mutht be amuthed, Thquire, thomehow; ... they
can't be alwayth a working, nor yet they can't be alwayth a
learning. Make the betht of uth, not the wurtht.'
Charles Dickens, *Hard Times* (Mr Sleary)

There are people who can do all fine and heroic things but
one: keep from telling their happiness to the unhappy.
Mark Twain, *Following the Equator*

'Fan the sinking flame of hilarity with the wing of friendship;
and pass the rosy wine.'
Charles Dickens, *Old Curiosity Shop* (Swiveller)

We all strive for happiness, but what would happiness be
if it clung to us like a poor relation?
Somerset Maugham, Attrib.

The truth is, I do indulge myself a little the more pleasure,
knowing that this is the proper age of my life to do it, and out
of my observation that most men that do thrive in the world
do forget to take pleasure during the time that they are getting
their estate but reserve that till they have got one, and then it
is too late for the to enjoy it with any pleasure.
Samuel Pepys, *The Diary of Samuel Pepys*, 10 March 1666

Pleasure will be paid, one time or another.
WILLIAM SHAKESPEARE, *Twelfth Night*

Happiness is never my aim ... I have neither time nor taste for such comas, attainable at the price of a pipeful of opium or a glass of whiskey.
GEORGE BERNARD SHAW, *Sixteen Self Sketches*

> I looked, I stared, I smiled, I laughed; and all
> The weight of sadness was in wonder lost.
> WILLIAM WORDSWORTH, *Miscellaneous Sonnets*

Nothing is so pleasant as to think of the sacrifices that one will never have to make.
SOMERSET MAUGHAM, Attrib.

Hope is itself a species of happiness and perhaps, the chief happiness in which this world affords; but, like other pleasures immoderately enjoyed, the excess of hope must be expiated by pain.
DR JOHNSON, Attrib.

While the laughter of *joy* is in full harmony with our deeper life, the laughter of amusement should be kept apart from it.
LEWIS CARROLL, *Life and Letters*

Happiness seeks obscurity to enjoy itself.
MARK TWAIN, Attrib.

A cigarette is the perfect type of perfect pleasure.
It is exquisite, and it leaves one unsatisfied.
What more could one want?
OSCAR WILDE, *The Picture of Dorian Gray*

The happiness that a generous spirit derives from the belief
that it exists in others is often greater
than the primary happiness itself.
THOMAS HARDY, *Desperate Remedies*

The more you reach after the fatal flower of happiness, which
trembles so blue and lovely in a crevice just beyond your
grasp, the more fearfully you become aware of the ghastly
and awful gulf of the precipice below you, into which you
will inevitably plunge, as into the bottomless pit,
if you reach any farther.
D. H. LAWRENCE, *The Fox*

'Like other great men under reverses,' he added with a smile,
'I must endeavour to subdue my mind to my fortune.
I must learn to brook being happier than I deserve.'
JANE AUSTEN, *Persuasion* (Captain Wentworth)

I forget who it was that recommended men for their soul's
good to do each day two things they disliked ... it is a precept
that I have followed scrupulously; for every day I have got up
and I have gone to bed.
SOMERSET MAUGHAM, Attrib.

[After dining with a group of wits]
They only served to convince me how superior humour is to
wit in respect to enjoyment – These men say things which
make one start, without making one feel ...
JOHN KEATS, Letter to George and Thomas Keats, December 1817

What is title, what is treasure,
What is reputation's care?
If we lead a life of pleasure,
`Tis no matter how or where!
ROBERT BURNS, 'The Jolly Beggars'

I hate ecstasy, Dionysic or any other.
It's like going round in a squirrel cage.
D. H. LAWRENCE, *Women in Love*

Grief can take care of itself; but to get the full value of
a joy you must have somebody to divide it with.
MARK TWAIN, *Following the Equator*

The irresistible, universal, automatic tendency
to find sweet pleasure somewhere, which pervades all life,
from the meanest to the highest.
THOMAS HARDY, *Tess of the d'Urbervilles*

Real laughter is a night as rare as real tears.
SIR WALTER SCOTT, *The Journal of Sir Walter Scott*

I am a Coward, I cannot bear the pain of being happy ...
JOHN KEATS, Letter to Fanny Brawne, September 1819

'I am happier even than Jane; she only smiles, I laugh.'
JANE AUSTEN, *Pride and Prejudice* (Elizabeth Bennet)

I am never more tickled than when I laugh at myself.
MARK TWAIN, Attrib.

Mankind are always happy for having been happy; so that if
you make them happy now, you make them happy twenty
years hence by the memory of it.
SYDNEY SMITH, *Sketches of Moral Philosophy*

I adore simple pleasures.
They are the last refuge of the complex.
OSCAR WILDE, *A Woman of No Importance*

The chief pleasure connected with asking an opinion
lies in not adopting it.
THOMAS HARDY, *Desperate Remedies*

We lose half the pleasure we might have in life,
by not really attending.
LEWIS CARROLL, *Sylvie and Bruno*

Nothing like a little judicious levity.
ROBERT LOUIS STEVENSON, *The Wrecker*

Despondency and Solitude

When sorrows come they come not single spies
But in battalions.
WILLIAM SHAKESPEARE, *Hamlet*

Solitude is the climax of the negative virtues.
ROBERT LOUIS STEVENSON, 'Reflections and Remarks on Human Life'

A man can no longer be private and withdrawn. The world
allows no hermits.
D. H. LAWRENCE, *Lady Chatterley's Lover*

Being alone in body and spirit begets loneliness,
and loneliness begets more loneliness.
F. SCOTT FITZGERALD, *Tender is the Night*

I did not know it was possible to be so miserable and live.
EVELYN WAUGH, *Letters*

The world does not despise us; it only neglects us.
THOMAS HARDY, *Life*

It is a depressing thought to be a shrill relic at the age of
fifty-two, but there is still a little time left,
and I may yet snap out of it.
NOËL COWARD, British press, 1952

What a strange scene if the surge of conversation could
suddenly ebb like the tide and show us the state of people's
real minds ...
No eyes the rocks discover
Which lurk beneath the deep.
Life could not be endured were it seen in reality.
SIR WALTER SCOTT, *The Journal of Sir Walter Scott*

> That inward eye
> Which is the bliss of solitude.
> WILLIAM WORDSWORTH, 'I Wandered Lonely as a Cloud'

Human life seems, on the whole, to contain more of sorrow
than of joy. And yet the world goes on. Who knows why?
LEWIS CARROLL, *Sylvie and Bruno Concluded*

Whatever be the misery to be endured, get it over.
The horror of every agony is in its anticipation.
ANTHONY TROLLOPE, *Way We Live Now*

> Hating the night when I couldn't sleep and
> hating the day because it went towards night.
> F. SCOTT FITZGERALD, *The Crack-Up*

You cannot conceive what a delightful companion you are
now you are gone.
LORD BYRON, Letter to Hobhouse, 1810

[89]

I like people to be unhappy because I like them to have souls.
We all have, doubtless, but I like the suffering soul
which confesses itself. I distrust this hard, this shiny,
this enamelled content.
VIRGINIA WOOLF, Letter, 22 September 1926

The most irksome of solitude is not the solitude of
remoteness, but that which is just outside desirable company.
THOMAS HARDY, *The Woodlanders*

The love of solitude increases by indulgence.
SIR WALTER SCOTT, *The Journal of Sir Walter Scott*

Solitude is dangerous to reason,
without being favourable to virtue.
DR JOHNSON, *Johnsonian Miscellanies*

Everybody is haunted with spectres and apparitions of sorrow,
and the imaginary griefs of life are greater than the real.
Whatever the English zenith may be, the horizon is
almost always of a sombre colour.
SYDNEY SMITH, Letter, 1819

The best laid schemes o' mice and men
Gang aft agley,
And lea'e us nought but grief an' pain,
For promised joy
ROBERT BURNS, 'To a Mouse'

A time comes when men laugh at misery through long acquaintance with it.
THOMAS HARDY, *The Return of the Native*

Let other pens dwell on guilt and misery. I quit such odious subjects as soon as I can.
JANE AUSTEN, *Mansfield Park*

So much has happened to me lately that I despair of even assimilating it – or forgetting it, which is the same thing.
F. SCOTT FITZGERALD, *The Letters*, 18 April 1927

Despair ruins some, Presumption many.
BENJAMIN FRANKLIN, *Poor Richard's Almanack*

Man is of dust: ethereal hopes are his.
WILLIAM WORDSWORTH, *The Excursion*

When we our betters see bearing our woes
We scarcely think our miseries our foes.
Who alone suffers, suffers most in the mind.
WILLIAM SHAKESPEARE, *King Lear*

Very few of the people who accentuate the futility of life remark the futility of themselves.
F. SCOTT FITZGERALD, *The Beautiful and Damned*

I do not know that I am happiest when alone; but this I am
sure of, that I never am long in the society even of *her* I love,
(God knows too well, and the devil probably too) without
a yearning for the company of my lamp and my utterly
confused and tumbled-over library.

LORD BYRON, *Journal*, 1813

The sensitiveness of habitual solitude makes hearts beat for
preternaturally small reasons.

THOMAS HARDY, *The Trumpet-Major*

O Life! thou art a galling load,
Along a rough, a weary road,
To wretches such as I!

ROBERT BURNS, 'Despondency – an Ode'

You tell me never to despair – I wish it was as easy for me
to observe the saying – truth is I have a horrid Morbidity of
Temperament which has shown itself at intervals ... it is I
have no doubt the greatest Enemy ... I have to fear.

JOHN KEATS, Letter to B.R. Haydon, May 1817

Misery taught him nothing more than defiant endurance of it.

THOMAS HARDY, *The Mayor of Casterbridge*

I can see nothing objectionable in the total destruction of the
earth, provided it is done, as seems most likely, inadvertently.

EVELYN WAUGH, *Essays*

The solitary mortal is certainly luxurious,
probably superstitious, and possibly mad.
DR JOHNSON, *Johnsonian Miscellanies*

I don't care so much for solitude as I used to:
results, I suppose, of marriage.
ROBERT LOUIS STEVENSON, Letter to Charles Baxter, December 1881

The other day I was asked why a certain man did not live
at Boar's Hill, the pleasant neighbourhood where so many
writers live, and replied, 'We Anglo-Irish hate to surrender
the solitude we have inherited', and then began to wonder
what I meant. I ran over the lines of my friends, of Swift
and Berkeley, and saw that all, as befits scattered men in an
ignorant country, were solitaries.
W. B YEATS, Attrib.

Nothing dies so hard and rallies so often as intolerance.
SYDNEY SMITH, *Edinburgh Review*, 1811

If the question was eternal company without the power of
retiring within yourself or solitary confinement for life I
should say 'Turnkey, lock the cell'.
SIR WALTER SCOTT, *The Journal of Sir Walter Scott*

All is lost save memory.
F. SCOTT FITZGERALD, 'My Lost City'

Writing, Art and Culture

An author who talks about his own books is almost as bad as a
mother who talks about her own children.
BENJAMIN DISRAELI, Speech in Glasgow, 19 November 1873

Did you ever know a writer to calmly take a
just criticism and shut up?
F. SCOTT FITZGERALD, *The Letters*, 4 May 1925

No human being ever spoke of scenery for above two
minutes at a time, which makes me suspect we hear
too much of it in literature.
ROBERT LOUIS STEVENSON, 'The Day After Tomorrow'

Most writers fail from lack of character
rather than from lack of intelligence.
EZRA POUND, *ABC of Reading*

I'd like a language which is above all languages, a language to
which all will do service. I cannot express myself in English
without enclosing myself in a tradition.
JAMES JOYCE, *Letters of James Joyce*, 12 July 1905

Novelists should never allow themselves to weary of the study
of real life – If they observed this duty conscientiously, they
would give us fewer pictures chequered with vivid contrasts of
light and shade.
CHARLOTTE BRONTË, *The Professor*

I am convinced more and more that fine writing is next to
fine doing, the top thing in the world ...
JOHN KEATS, Letter to Benjamin Bailey, August 1819

I do not pretend to be a philosopher, but merely a man who
has throughout his life been profoundly interested in art.
SOMERSET MAUGHAM, Attrib.

I quite agree with you as to the horrors of correspondence.
Correspondences are like small-clothes before the invention
of suspenders: it is impossible to keep them up.
SYDNEY SMITH, Letter, 1841

The best of every author is in general to be found in his book.
DR JOHNSON, *Johnsonian Miscellanies*

I would rather be an artist than a careerist.
F. SCOTT FITZGERALD, *The Letters*, 23 April 1934

The regular resource of people who don't go enough into the
world to live a novel is to write one.
THOMAS HARDY, *A Pair of Blue Eyes*

I don't believe the artist who sets to work to create a work of
art has any such purpose as aesthetes ascribe to him. If he has,
he is didactic or a propagandist, and as such not an artist.
SOMERSET MAUGHAM, Attrib.

Of all the Arts the one most to be recommended to the young beginner is literature. Painting is messy; music is noisy; and the applied arts and crafts all require a certain amount of skill. But writing is clean, quiet, and can be done anywhere at any time by anyone.

EVELYN WAUGH, *Essays*

'But romance-writers might know nothing of love, judging by the way in which they treat of it.'

CHARLOTTE BRONTË, *Shirley*, II (Caroline Helstone)

In literature as in love courage is half the battle.

SIR WALTER SCOTT, *The Journal of Sir Walter Scott*

Fashion is what one wears oneself. What is unfashionable is what other people wear.

OSCAR WILDE, *An Ideal Husband*

'*Classic.*' A book which people praise and don't read.

MARK TWAIN, *Following the Equator*

I own the most delightful habit in the world, the habit of reading, thus providing myself with a refuge from all the distresses of life.

SOMERSET MAUGHAM, Attrib.

Great Art is *never* popular to start with.

EZRA POUND, *Letters*, 1917

I believe that literature is the principle voice of the conscience, and it is its duty age after age to affirm its morality against the specific moralities of clergymen and churches; and of kings and parliaments and peoples.
W. B. YEATS, Letter to the Editor of the *Freeman's Journal*, 14 November 1901

I make it a rule to cheat nobody but Booksellers, a race on whom I have no mercy.
SIR WALTER SCOTT, *The Letters of Sir Walter Scott*

Memoirs are true and useful stars, whilst studied histories are those stars joined in constellations, according to the fancy of the poet.
SAMUEL PEPYS, *Samuel Pepys's Naval Minutes*

The business of the poet and novelist is to show the sorriness underlying the grandest things, and the grandeur underlying the sorriest things.
THOMAS HARDY, *Life*

Books are good enough in their own way, but they are a mighty bloodless substitute for life.
ROBERT LOUIS STEVENSON, 'An Apology for Idlers'

Men will forgive a man anything except bad prose.
WINSTON CHURCHILL, Speech in Manchester, 1906

To write it, it took three months;
to conceive it – three minutes;
to collect the data on it – all my life.
F. SCOTT FITZGERALD, *The Letters*, April 1920

As a novelist, I feel it is the change inside the individual
which is my real concern. The great social change interests me
and troubles me, but it is not my field … My field is to know
the feelings inside a man, and to make new feelings conscious.
D. H. LAWRENCE, *The State of Funk*

Great literature is simply language charged with meaning
to the utmost possible degree.
EZRA POUND, *Literature Essays*

'The usual style of letter-writing among women is faultless,
except in three particulars.'
'And what are they?'
'A general deficiency of subject, a total inattention to stops,
and a very frequent ignorance of grammar.'
JANE AUSTEN, *Northanger Abbey*
(Henry Tilney and Catherine Morland)

But I do feel myself that I ought to have been able to make
not merely thousands of people interested in literature;
but millions.
VIRGINIA WOOLF, *A Writer's Diary*, 24 August 1940

A good painter has two chief objects to paint: namely, man
and the intention of his soul.
SOMERSET MAUGHAM, Attrib.

Acting is not a state of *being* ... but a state of appearing to be.
You can't be eight times a week without going stark
staring mad. You've got to be in control.
NOËL COWARD, *Sunday Times*, 1964

Hemingway avoids New York, for he has the most valuable
asset an artist can possess – the fear of what he knows is bad
for him.
DOROTHY PARKER, Attrib.

The artist, like the God of the creation, remains within or
behind or beyond or above his handiwork, invisible, refined
out of existence, indifferent, paring his fingernails.
JAMES JOYCE, *A Portrait of the Artist as a Young Man*

Having once found the intensity of art, nothing else that
can happen in life can ever again seem as important as the
creative process.
F. SCOTT FITZGERALD, *The Letters*

Is there no play
To ease the anguish of a torturing hour?
WILLIAM SHAKESPEARE, *A Midsummer Night's Dream*

A writer must feel and think, he must read, and he must put
himself in the way of gaining experience.
SOMERSET MAUGHAM, Attrib.

Perhaps the hardest thing in all literature – at least *I* have
found it so: by no voluntary effort can I accomplish it:
I have to take it as it comes – is to write anything *original*.
And perhaps the easiest is, when once an original line has
been struck out, to follow it up, and to write any amount
more to the same tune.
LEWIS CARROLL, *Sylvie and Bruno*

You will learn a great deal of virtue by studying any art;
but nothing of any art in the study of virtue.
ROBERT LOUIS STEVENSON, 'Reflections and Remarks on Human life'

Every great and original writer, in proportion as he is great
and original, must himself create the taste by which he is to
be relished.
WILLIAM WORDSWORTH, *Lyrical Ballads*

Literature is news that STAYS news.
EZRA POUND, *ABC of Reading*

Fancy [imagination] is a gift which the owner of it cannot
measure, and the power of which, when he is using it,
he cannot himself understand.
ANTHONY TROLLOPE, *Thackeray*

All good art is experience; all popular bad art generalisation.
W. B. YEATS, Journal, August 1910

There are few books to which some objection
or other may not be made.
DR JOHNSON, Attrib.

Humility is not a virtue propitious to the artist. It is often
pride, emulation, avarice, malice – all odious qualities – which
drive a man to complete, elaborate, refine, destroy, renew, his
work until he has made something that gratifies his pride and
envy and greed. And in doing so he enriches the world more
than the generous and good, though he may lose his own soul
in the process. That is the paradox of artistic achievement.
EVELYN WAUGH, Essays

The good ended happily, the bad unhappily.
That is what Fiction means.
OSCAR WILDE, The Importance of Being Earnest

I never saw an author who was aware that there was any
dimensional difference between a fact and a surmise.
MARK TWAIN, My Father

Without art the crudeness of reality would make
the world unbearable.
GEORGE BERNARD SHAW, Back to Methuselah

If you are going to make a book end badly, it must end badly from the beginning.

ROBERT LOUIS STEVENSON, Letter to James Barrie, November 1892

In my heart of hearts I have never been quite certain that one
should be more than an artist, that even patriotism
is more than an impure desire in an artist.

W. B. YEATS, *What is Popular Poetry?*

Your letter is come; it came indeed twelve lines ago, but I could not stop to acknowledge it before, and I am glad it did not arrive till I had completed my first sentence, because the sentence had been made ever since yesterday, and I think forms a very good beginning.

JANE AUSTEN, *Letters*, 1 November 1800

I have come to the conclusion that I
cannot write without offending people.

JAMES JOYCE, Letter, 5 May 1906

Writing a book was an adventure. To begin with it was a toy, an amusement; then it became a mistress, and then a master, and then a tyrant.

WINSTON CHURCHILL, Speech in London, 2 November 1949

Scribbling [is] a disease I hope myself cured of.

LORD BYRON, Letter to His Mother, 1811

Writers aren't people exactly. Or, if they're any good, they're a whole *lot* of people trying so hard to be one person.

F. Scott Fitzgerald, *The Last Tycoon*

—

Critics – appalled, I venture on the name;
Those cut-throat bandits in the paths of fame:
Bloody dissectors, worse than ten Munroes,
He hacks to teach, they mangle to expose.

Robert Burns, 'Second Epistle to Robert Graham'

—

There is no such thing as a moral or an immoral book.
Books are well written, or badly written. That is all.

Oscar Wilde, *The Picture of Dorian Gray*

—

The radio and the film are mere counterfeit emotion all the time, the current press and literature the same. People wallow in emotion: counterfeit emotion. They lap it up: they live in and on it. They ooze with it.

D. H. Lawrence, *A Propos of 'Lady Chatterley's Lover'*

—

In writing the important thing is less richness of material than richness of personality.

Somerset Maugham, Attrib.

—

In this work [*The Rape of the Lock*] are exhibited, in a very high degree, the two most engaging powers of an author. New things are made familiar, and familiar things are made new.

Dr Johnson, *The Lives of the Poets*

When I want to read a novel I write one.
BENJAMIN DISRAELI, Attrib.

When I write I am merely a sensibility.
VIRGINIA WOOLF, *A Writer's Diary*, 22 August 1922

Literature is the right use of language irrespective of the subject or reason of the utterance. A political speech may be, and sometimes is, literature; a sonnet to the moon may be, and often is, trash.
EVELYN WAUGH, *Essays*

It would concern the reader little, perhaps, to know, how sorrowfully the pen is laid down at the close of a two-years' imaginative task; or how an Author feels as if he were dismissing some portion of himself into the shadowy world, when a crowd of the creatures of his brain are going from him for ever.
CHARLES DICKENS, *David Copperfield*

'The person, be it gentleman or lady, who has not pleasure in a good novel, must be intolerably stupid.'
JANE AUSTEN, *Northanger Abbey* (Henry Tilney)

Men would be more cautious of losing their time in [criticism], if they did but consider that to answer a book effectually requires more pains and skill, more wit, learning, and judgment than were employed in the writing it.
JONATHAN SWIFT, *A Tale of a Tub*

Fame depends on literature not on architecture. We are more eager to see a broken column of Cicero's villa than all those mighty labours of barbaric power [in different parts of India].
SIR WALTER SCOTT, *The Journal of Sir Walter Scott*

A good writer should be so simple that
he has no faults, only sins.
W. B. YEATS, Journal, October 1914

The true picture of life as it is, if it could be adequately painted, would show men what they are, and how they might rise, not, indeed, to perfection, but one step first, and then another on the ladder.
ANTHONY TROLLOPE, *Eustace Diamonds*

Length is no commendation to a letter from him that has
nothing to do to you that have a great deal.
SAMUEL PEPYS,
Private Correspondence and Miscellaneous Papers of Samuel Pepys

If it weren't for painting, I could not live; I could not bear the strain of things.
WINSTON CHURCHILL, Attrib.

The slowest and most intermittent talker must *seem* fluent in letter-writing. He may have taken half-an-hour to compose his second sentence; but there it is, close after the first!
LEWIS CARROLL, *Sylvie and Bruno Concluded*

One should read everything, More than half of modern
culture depends on what one shouldn't read.
OSCAR WILDE, *The Importance of Being Earnest*

No less than twenty-two publishers and printers read the
manuscript of *Dubliners* and when at last it was printed some
very kind person bought out the entire edition and had it
burnt in Dublin.
JAMES JOYCE, Letter, 2 April 1932

I don't read the *New Yorker* much these days.
It always seems to be the same old story about
somebody's childhood in Pakistan.
DOROTHY PARKER, Attrib.

Pay no attention to the criticism of men who have
never themselves written a notable work.
EZRA POUND, *Literary Essays*

It is strange that there should be so little reading in the world,
and so much writing. People in general do not willingly read,
if they can have anything else to amuse them.
DR JOHNSON, Attrib.

I do not think Shakespeare without the grossest of faults.
LORD BYRON, Letter to Octavius Gilchrist, 1821

Masterpieces exalt and refine and inspire, but their constant
proximity can become oppressive.
EVELYN WAUGH, *Essays*

All art is gratuitous; and the will to produce it,
like the will to live, must be held to justify itself.
GEORGE BERNARD SHAW, *The Saturday Review,* 2 April 1898

The main question as to a novel is, did it amuse? were you
surprised at dinner coming so soon? did you mistake eleven
for ten, and twelve for eleven? were you too late to dress? and
did you sit up beyond the usual hour? If a novel produces
these effects, it is good; if it does not – story, language, love,
scandal itself cannot save it. It is only meant to please; and it
must do that, or it does nothing.
SYDNEY SMITH, *Edinburgh Review,* 1813

After writing for fifteen years it struck me
I had no talent for writing. I couldn't give it up.
By that time I was already famous.
MARK TWAIN, *The Twainian,* May-June 1952

All writing is nothing but putting words on
the backs of rhythm.
VIRGINIA WOOLF, Letter, 7 April 1930

You know who the critics are?
The men who have failed in literature and art.
BENJAMIN DISRAELI, *Lothair*

[109]

There seems almost a general wish of decrying the capacity
and undervaluing the labour of the novelist, and of slighting
the performances which have only genius, wit, and taste to
recommend them.
JANE AUSTEN, *Northanger Abbey*

My art is not a mirror held up to nature.
Nature mirrors my art.
JAMES JOYCE, Attrib.

Read much, but not many books.
BENJAMIN FRANKLIN, *Poor Richard's Almanack*

As a general rule, run your pen through every other word
you have written; you have no idea what vigour it
will give your style.
SYDNEY SMITH, *Memoir*

Like the cobra and the mongoose, the artist and the critic
have always been and will be Nature's irreconcilables.
NOËL COWARD, *Sunday Times*, 29 January 1961

Words are too awful an instrument for good and evil,
to be trifled with, they hold above all other external
powers a dominion over thoughts.
WILLIAM WORDSWORTH, 'The Dominion of Words'

There is no great nationality without literature, no great
literature without nationality.
W. B. Yeats, 'The Celt in London'

Knowledge is *not* culture. The domain of culture begins when
one *has* 'forgotten-what-book'.
Ezra Pound, *Guide to Kulchur*

No great artist ever sees things as they really are.
If he did he would cease to be an artist.
Oscar Wilde, *The Decay of Lying*

When I get to heaven I mean to spend a considerable
portion of my first million years in painting,
and so get to the bottom of the subject.
Winston Churchill, *Thoughts and Adventures*

Certainly nobody wants to complain about sex itself; but
I think we all have a legitimate grievance in the fact that,
as it is shown in present-day novels, its practitioners are so
unmercifully articulate about it ... There is no more cruel
destroyer of excitement than painstaking detail. Who reads
these play-by-play reports of passion responds with much
the same thrill as he would experience in looking over the
blueprints for some stranger's garage.
Dorothy Parker, Attrib.

Art is the first luxury to be discarded in times of stress; the artist is the first of the workers to suffer. But intellectually also he depends upon society. Society is not only his paymaster but his patron.

VIRGINIA WOOLF, *The Moment and Other Essays*

The first duty of an author is, I conceive, a faithful allegiance to Truth and Nature.

CHARLOTTE BRONTË, Letter to W. S. Williams, 14 August 1848

A work of art is not a matter of thinking beautiful thoughts or experiencing tender emotions (though those are its raw materials), but of intelligence, skill, taste, proportion, knowledge, discipline and industry; especially discipline. No number of disciples can compensate for lack of that.

EVELYN WAUGH, *Letters*, 1960

There is no sovereign in the republic of letters; and even if there were, I have never had the pretension or the power to become a usurper.

LORD BYRON, Letter to J. J. Coulmann, 1823

The novel ... was the strongest and supplest medium for conveying thought and emotion from one human being to another.

F. SCOTT FITZGERALD, *The Crack-Up*

If *Hamlet* and *Oedipus* were published now, they wouldn't sell
more than 100 copies, unless they were pushed.
D. H. Lawrence, Letter to Edward Garnett, 1913

Plato said that artists ought to be kept out of the ideal
republic, and the artists swore by their gods that
nothing would drag them into it.
Ezra Pound, *Literary Essays*

When a man writes from his own mind, he writes very
rapidly. The greatest part of a writer's time is spent
in reading, in order to write: a man will turn over
half a library to make one book.
Dr Johnson, Attrib.

The true ambition is to make criticism as international,
and literature as National as possible.
W. B. Yeats, Letter to the Editor of *United Ireland*, 1894

Books are fatal; they are the curse of the human race.
Nine-tenths of existing books are nonsense and the clever
books are the refutation of that nonsense.
Benjamin Disraeli, *Lothair*

I thought to myself: Thank God, I can look at a sunset now
without having to think how to describe it. I meant then
never to write another book.
Somerset Maugham, Attrib.

[113]

I think the business of art is ... not to show, by a backward light, what everything has been working to – but only to *suggest*, until the fulfilment comes. These are the ways of Providence, of which ways all art is but a little imitation.
CHARLES DICKENS, Letter to Wilkie Collins, 6 October 1859

When I am writing for myself for the mere sake of the Moment's enjoyment, perhaps Nature has its course with me – but a Preface is written to the Public, a thing I cannot help looking upon as an Enemy ...
JOHN KEATS, Letter to J.H. Reynolds, April 1818

No furniture so charming as books, even if you never open them, or read a single word.
SYDNEY SMITH, *Memoir*

I am James Joyce. I understand that you are to translate *Ulysses*, and I have come from Paris to tell you not to alter a single word.
JAMES JOYCE, Attrib.

'Shakespeare one gets acquainted with without knowing how. It is part of an Englishman's constitution.'
JANE AUSTEN, *Mansfield Park*, III (Henry Crawford)

Art never expresses anything but itself.
OSCAR WILDE, *The Decay of Lying*

Any man of real individuality tries to know and to understand what is happening, even in himself, as he goes along. This struggle for verbal consciousness should not be left out in art. It is a very great part of life. It is not superimposition of a theory. It is the passionate struggle into conscious being.

D. H. LAWRENCE, *Women in Love*

There are only two passions in art; there are only love and hate – with endless modifications.

EZRA POUND, *Literary Essays*

I know nothing taken from the sea into common use among people of quality but the word *Huzzah*, and whence comes that, and how laudably applied?

SAMUEL PEPYS, *Samuel Pepys's Naval Minutes*

What kind of talent is required to please this mighty public? That was my first question, and was soon amended with the words, 'if any'.

ROBERT LOUIS STEVENSON, 'Popular Authors'

Words mean more than we mean to express when we use them; so a whole book ought to mean a great deal more than the writer means.

LEWIS CARROLL, *Life and Letters*

My books are water: those of the great geniuses are wine. Everybody drinks water.

MARK TWAIN, *Notebook*

An author ought to write for the youth of his own
generation, the critics of the next, and the schoolmasters of
ever afterward.
F. Scott Fitzgerald, *The Letters*, April 1920

Here I come to one of the memoir writer's difficulties – one of
the reasons why, though I read so many, so many are failures.
They leave out the person to whom things happened. The
reason is that it is so difficult to describe any human being.
Virginia Woolf, *Moments of Being*

Words which he did not understand he said over and over to
himself till he had learnt them by heart: and through them he
had glimpses of the real world about him.
James Joyce, *A Portrait of the Artist as a Young Man*

A third rogue writes to tell me ... that he approves of the first
three volumes of the *Heart of Midlothian* but totally
condemns the fourth ... However an author should
be reasonably well pleased when three fourths of his works
are acceptable to the reader.
Sir Walter Scott, *The Journal of Sir Walter Scott*

The new playwrights invent their subjects and dislike
anything customary in the arrangement of the fable,
but their expression is as common as the newspapers where
they first learned to write.
W. B. Yeats, Journal, September 1909

I would rather be attacked than unnoticed. For the worst thing you can do to an author is to be silent as to his works.
DR JOHNSON, Attrib.

Certain books form a treasure, a basis, once read they will serve you for the rest of your lives.
EZRA POUND, *Guide to Kulchur*

Poetry and Music

If my Poems are inspired by Genius and Nature they will live, if not, they will be forgotten and the sooner the better.
WILLIAM WORDSWORTH, *Letters*

Poetry ... is the most concentrated form of style.
F. SCOTT FITZGERALD, *The Letters*, 29 July 1940

> Sure a poet is a sage;
> A humanist, physician to all men.
> JOHN KEATS, 'The Fall of Hyperion'

Poetry should only occupy the idle. In more serious affairs it would be ridiculous.
LORD BYRON, Conversation with Lady Blessington, 1823

> I do not understand or care about fine music but there is
> something in [Sandy Ballantyne's] violin
> which goes to the very heart.
> SIR WALTER SCOTT, *The Journal of Sir Walter Scott*

[Boswell] Then, Sir, what is poetry?
[Johnson] Why, Sir, it is much easier to say what it is not. We all *know* what light is; but it is not easy to tell what it is.
DR JOHNSON, Attrib.

To find beauty in ugliness is the province of the poet.
THOMAS HARDY, *Life*

The man that hath no music in himself,
Nor is not moved with concord of sweet sounds,
Is fit for treasons, stratagems, and spoils.
WILLIAM SHAKESPEARE, *The Merchant of Venice*

Poetry is about as much a 'criticism of life' as red-hot iron is a criticism of fire.
EZRA POUND, *The Spirit of Romance*

None but the best poetry will stand close
printing and cheap paper.
LEWIS CARROLL, Attrib.

Say my love is easy had,
Say I'm bitten raw with pride,
Say I am too often sad –
Still behold me at your side.
Say I'm neither brave nor young,
Say I woo and coddle care,
Say the devil touched my tongue –
Still you have my heart to wear.
But say my verses do not scan,
And I get me another man!
DOROTHY PARKER, 'Fighting Words'

Who mocks at music mocks at love.
W. B. YEATS, 'The Countess Cathleen'

Tennessee Williams has a strong streak of poetry, but I think he has run into the ground, rather – what with all those neurotic mothers, castrations and things.
NOËL COWARD, Attrib.

I wish that life were an opera. I should like to live in one; but I don't know in what quarter of the globe I shall find a society so constituted.
ROBERT LOUIS STEVENSON, Letter to Mrs Thomas Stevenson, August 1872

'I consider music as a very innocent diversion, and perfectly compatible with the profession of a clergyman.'
JANE AUSTEN, *Pride and Prejudice* (Mr Collins)

The only sensual pleasure without vice [music].
DR JOHNSON, *Johnsonian Miscellanies*

After playing Chopin, I feel as if I had been weeping over sins that I had never committed, and mourning over tragedies that were not my own.
OSCAR WILDE, *The Critic as Artist*

If Galileo had said in verse that the world moved, the Inquisition might have let him alone.
THOMAS HARDY, *Life*

No man ever writes very much poetry that 'matters'.
Ezra Pound, *Literary Essays*

I think it is time we made up our minds that poetry is one of the arts which has died in the last eighty years. Poets now have as much connection with poetry as the Fishmongers' Company has with selling fish. They carry on the name and the banquets but have retired from trade generations ago.
Evelyn Waugh, Attrib.

For ne'er
Was flattery lost on poet's ear:
A simple race! they waste their toil
For the vain tribute of a smile.
Sir Walter Scott, *The Lay of the Last Minstrel*

Poetry is the art of combining pleasure with truth, by calling imagination to the help of reason.
Dr Johnson, *The Lives of the Poets*

By the common consent of all mankind who have read, poetry takes the highest place in literature.
Anthony Trollope, *Autobiography*

The voice which is the voice of my poetry, without imagination, cannot be heard.
William Wordsworth, *Letters*

Like all poets I have a passion for pugilism.
GEORGE BERNARD SHAW, *How He Lied to Her Husband*

Prose wanders around with a lantern and laboriously
schedules and verifies the details and particulars of a valley
and its frame of crags and peaks, then Poetry comes, and lays
bare the whole landscape with a single splendid flash.
MARK TWAIN, Attrib.

Words are always getting conventionalised to some secondary
meaning. It is one of the works of poetry to take the truants
in custody and bring them back to their right senses. Poets are
the policemen of language, they are always arresting those old
reprobates the words.
W. B. YEATS, Letter to Ellen O'Leary, 1889

> Music oft hath such a charm
> To make bad good, and good provoke harm.
> WILLIAM SHAKESPEARE, *Measure for Measure*

[Dryden] has often said to me in confidence, that the world
would have never suspected him to be so great a poet, if he
had not assured them so frequently in his Prefaces that it was
impossible they could either doubt or forget it.
JONATHAN SWIFT, *A Tale of a Tub*

Long poems can be popular *provided they aren't too poetic*.
EZRA POUND, *Letters*, 1915

One poet should always speak for another.
SIR WALTER SCOTT, *The Journal of Sir Walter Scott*

This leads me onto another axiom. That if Poetry comes not
as naturally as the Leaves to a tree
it had better not come at all.
JOHN KEATS, Letter to John Taylor, February 1818

Beauty is the end and law of poetry.
W. B. YEATS, Letter to George Russell (AE), 1900

In sweet music is such art
Killing care and grief of heart.
WILLIAM SHAKESPEARE, *Henry VIII*

I take up books, and fling them down again. I began a
comedy, and burnt it because the scene ran into *reality*;
– a novel, for the same reason. In rhyme, I can keep
more away from facts.
LORD BYRON, *Journal*, 1813

The poet is one who enters and mounts a platform to give an
address as announced. He opens his page, looks around,
and finds the hall – empty.
THOMAS HARDY, *Life*

About the beginning of the seventeenth century appeared a race of writers that may be termed the *metaphysical poets* ... [they] were men of learning, and to show their learning was their sole endeavour; but, unluckily resolving to show it in rhyme, instead of writing poetry they only wrote verses.
DR JOHNSON, Attrib.

Music makes one feel so romantic – at least it always gets on one's nerves.
OSCAR WILDE, *A Woman of No Importance*

Poetry is the safeguard of my passions, but I wish to act what I write.
BENJAMIN DISRAELI, Attrib.

Drama is the poetry of conduct, romance the poetry of circumstance.
ROBERT LOUIS STEVENSON, 'Gossip on Romance'

How full of grace and invention is Mozart after the muscle-bound Beethoven.
JAMES JOYCE, Attrib.

Poetry is either something that lives like fire inside you – like music to the musician or Marxism to the Communist – or else it is nothing, an empty, formalized bore around which pedants can endlessly drone their notes and explanations.
F. SCOTT FITZGERALD, *The Letters*, 3 August 1940

The magic of music is in its effect on volition. A sudden clearing of the mind of rubbish and the re-establishment of a sense of proportion.

EZRA POUND, *Guide to Kulchur*

All animated Nature loves music – except myself!

DR JOHNSON, Attrib.

We make out of the quarrel with others, rhetoric, but out of the quarrel with ourselves, poetry.

W. B. YEATS, 'Per Amica Silentia Luna'

I don't wonder, that, in dismissing all the other deities of Paganism, the Muse should have been retained by common consent; for, in sober reality, writing good verses seems to depend upon something separate from the volition of the author.

SIR WALTER SCOTT, *The Letters of Sir Walter Scott*

'I have been used to consider poetry as the food of love,' said Darcy.
'Of a fine, stout, healthy love it may. Every thing nourishes what is strong already. But if it be only a slight thin sort of inclination, I am convinced that one good sonnet will starve it entirely away.'

JANE AUSTEN, *Pride and Prejudice* (Elizabeth Bennet and Mr Darcy)

Humanly speaking, it is a more important matter to play the fiddle, even badly, than to write huge works upon recondite subjects.
ROBERT LOUIS STEVENSON, 'Steerage Scenes'

The fact is, there are no rules, and there never were any rules, and there never will be any rules of musical composition except rules of thumb; and thumbs vary in length, like ears.
GEORGE BERNARD SHAW, Attrib.

My thirst and passion from boyhood ... has been for poetry – for poetry in its widest and wildest sense – for poetry untrammelled by the laws of sense, rhyme, or rhythm, soaring through the universe, and echoing the music of the spheres.
LEWIS CARROLL, *Novelty and Romancement*

A poem: one of those genuine productions so often vouchsafed to the fortunate public of those days – the golden age of modern literature. Alas! the readers of our era are less favoured.
CHARLOTTE BRONTË, *Jane Eyre*, III

'Poetry's unnat'ral; no man ever talked in poetry 'cept a beadle on boxin' day, or Warren's blackin' or Rowland's oil, or some o' them low fellows.'
CHARLES DICKENS, *The Pickwick Papers* (Tony Weller)

Science is unpoetic only to minds jaundiced with sentiment
and romanticism.
EZRA POUND, Attrib.

I have taken to cooking and listening to Wagner,
both of which frighten me to death.
NOËL COWARD, *The Noël Coward Diaries,* 19 February 1956

Poetry is the breath and finer spirit of all knowledge; it is the
impassioned expression which is in the countenance of all
science.
WILLIAM WORDSWORTH, *Lyrical Ballads*

In Pope, I cannot read a line,
But with a sigh, I wish it mine:
When he can in one Couplet fix
More sense than I can do in six:
It gives me such a jealous fit,
I cry, 'Pox take him, and his wit.'
JONATHAN SWIFT, *Verses on the Death of Doctor Swift*

And I would have all know that when all falls
In ruin, poetry calls out in joy,
Being the scattering hand, the bursting pod,
The victim's joy among the holy flame,
God's laughter at the shattering of the world.
W. B. YEATS, 'The King's Threshold'

Music is perhaps the bridge between consciousness and the unthinking sentient or even insentient universe.

EZRA POUND, Attrib.

You know my high opinion of your own poetry, – because it is of *no* school.

LORD BYRON, Letter to Percy Bysshe Shelley, 1821

There is no greater Sin after the 7 deadly than to flatter oneself into an idea of being a great Poet.

JOHN KEATS, Letter to B. R. Haydon, May 1817

If one plays good music, people don't listen, and if one plays bad music people don't talk.

OSCAR WILDE, *The Importance of Being Earnest*

There is nothing of which Nature has been more bountiful than poets. They swarm like the spawn of cod-fish, with a vicious fecundity that incites and requires destruction. To publish verses is become a sort of evidence that a man wants sense; which is repelled not by writing good verses, but by writing excellent verses.

SYDNEY SMITH, *Edinburgh Review*, 1813

Musick, a science peculiarly productive of a pleasure that no
state of life, publick or private, secular or sacred; no difference
of age or season; no temper of mind or condition of health
exempt from present anguish; nor, lastly, distinction of
quality, renders either improper, untimely or unentertaining.
SAMUEL PEPYS,
Private Correspondence and Miscellaneous Papers of Samuel Pepys

The poet's eye, in a fine frenzy rolling,
Doth glance from heaven to earth, from earth to heaven,
And as imagination bodies forth
The forms of things unknown, the poet's pen
Turns them to shapes, and gives to airy nothing
A local habitation and a name.
WILLIAM SHAKESPEARE, *A Midsummer Night's Dream*

Human Nature

As I know more of mankind I expect less of them, and am
ready now to call a man *a good man*, upon easier terms than I
was formerly.
DR JOHNSON, Attrib.

Is aught so certain as that man is doomed
To breathe beneath a vault of ignorance?
WILLIAM WORDSWORTH, 'The Excursion'

But Man we find the only creature,
Who, led by Folly, fights with Nature.
JONATHAN SWIFT, 'On Poetry: A Rhapsody'

Man is a gregarious animal. We are members of a herd.
SOMERSET MAUGHAM, Attrib.

We watched little boys of nine and ten undressing and
dressing with such excessive modesty that it took them ages
to get their little wet bathing trunks off under their towels.
They squirmed and wriggled, contorting themselves into most
uncomfortable attitudes for fear that some roving eye might
chance momentarily on their poor little privates. What a
dreadful and foolish mistake to inculcate that
self-consciousness into small children. Oh dear.
We really are a most peculiar race.
NOËL COWARD, *The Noël Coward Diaries*, 1 July 1946

All the world's a stage,
And all the men and women merely players;
They have their exits and their entrances
And one man in his time plays many parts,
His acts being seven ages.
WILLIAM SHAKESPEARE, *As You Like It*

He who has never hoped can never despair.
GEORGE BERNARD SHAW, *Caesar and Cleopatra*

The human race consists of the dangerously insane and such
as are not.
MARK TWAIN, *Mark Twain's Notebook*

Sir, a desire of knowledge is the natural feeling of mankind;
and every human being, whose mind is not debauched, will
be willing to give all that he has to get knowledge.
DR JOHNSON, Attrib.

Every sin is our last; every 1st of January a remarkable
turning-point in our career.
ROBERT LOUIS STEVENSON, 'El Dorado'

'If one scheme of happiness fails, human nature turns to
another.'
JANE AUSTEN, *Mansfield Park*, I (Mrs Grant)

Man is least himself when he talks in his own person.
Give him a mask, and he will tell the truth.
OSCAR WILDE, *The Critic as Artist*

It is no use trying to sum people up. One must follow hints,
not exactly what is said, nor yet entirely what is done ...
VIRGINIA WOOLF, *Jacob's Room*

If one is interested in one's fellow beings – and that after all is
the first requisite of a novelist – one cannot neglect the study
of human nature in unfamiliar surroundings.
EVELYN WAUGH, *Essays*

[On hearing the door bell or telephone ringing]
'What fresh hell is this?
DOROTHY PARKER, Attrib.

I ... believe in predestination ... and in the depravity of the
human heart in general, and of my own in particular.
LORD BYRON, Conversation with Lady Blessington, 1823

Life is all a variorum,
We regard not how it goes;
Let them cant about decorum,
Who have character to lose.
ROBERT BURNS, 'The Jolly Beggars'

What is it that we all live upon but self-esteem? When we want praise it is only because praise enables us to think well of ourselves.

ANTHONY TROLLOPE, *He Knew He Was Right*

A man who was aware that there could be no honour and yet had honour, who knew the sophistry of courage and yet was brave.

F. SCOTT FITZGERALD, *The Beautiful and Damned*

I cannot help being afraid of encouraging emulation – it proves too often closely akin to envy.

WILLIAM WORDSWORTH, *Letters*

The man that smiles – that reads *The Times* – That goes to Christmas Pantomimes – Is capable of any crimes!

LEWIS CARROLL, *Phantasmagoria*

It is in self-sacrifice that man fulfils himself. It is in giving all he has to those who are near and dear to him that he solves the riddle of life and makes out of his poor little existence a thing of beauty.

SOMERSET MAUGHAM, Attrib.

The world is made up of a mass of people and a few individuals.

D. H. LAWRENCE, *The Plumed Serpent*

The fallacy of our self-love extends itself as wide as our interest or affections. Every man believes that mistresses are unfaithful, and patrons capricious; but he expects his own mistress, and his own patron.
DR JOHNSON, Attrib.

No might nor greatness in mortality
Can censure 'scape; back-wounding calumny
The whitest virtue strikes. What king so strong
Can tie the gall up in the slanderous tongue?
WILLIAM SHAKESPEARE, *Measure for Measure*

But that is the way we are made: we don't reason,
where we feel; we just feel.
MARK TWAIN, *Connecticut Yankee*

Call the world ... 'The vale of Soul-making.' There may be intelligence or sparks of the divinity in millions – but they are not Souls till they acquire identities, till each one is personally itself.
JOHN KEATS, Letter to George and Georgiana Keats, April 1819

As a guide to human character, pedigrees are, I suppose, about as valuable as horoscopes.
EVELYN WAUGH, *Essays*

Conceit is an outward manifestation of inferiority.
NOËL COWARD, *The Times*, 1969

The people who get on in this world are the people who get up and look for the circumstances they want, and, if they can't find them, make them.

GEORGE BERNARD SHAW, *Mrs Warren's Profession*

What one wants to know is not what people did, but why they did it, or rather why they thought they did it; and to learn that, you should go to the men themselves. Their very falsehood is often more than another man's truth.

ROBERT LOUIS STEVENSON, Letter to Maud Babington, Summer 1871

There have been many great men that have flattered the people, who ne'er loved them; and there be many that they have loved, they know not wherefore. So that if they love they know not why, they hate upon no better a ground.

WILLIAM SHAKESPEARE, *Coriolanus*

And therefore by the way pray learne of mee this one Lesson, which on this Occasion I have Observed not onely you but others of Our Friends, not to have yet met with, vizt. To be most Slow to believe what we most wish should bee true.

SAMUEL PEPYS, *The Letters of Samuel Pepys and his Family Circle*

The truth is people scarcely care for each other. They have this insane instinct for life. But they never become attached to anything outside themselves.

VIRGINIA WOOLF, *A Writer's Diary*, 4 June 1923

There is no intelligence without emotion. There may be emotion without much intelligence, but that does not concern us.

EZRA POUND, *Literary Essays*

Thomas Gradgrind, sir ... With a rule and a pair of scales, and the multiplication table always in his pocket, sir, ready to weigh and measure any parcel of human nature, and tell you exactly what it comes to. It is a question of figures, a case of simple arithmetic.

CHARLES DICKENS, *Hard Times*

There lurks, perhaps, in every human heart a desire of distinction, which inclines every man first to hope, and then to believe, that Nature has given him something peculiar to himself.

DR JOHNSON, Attrib.

People live together in the same houses all their lives and at the end they are as far apart as ever.

JAMES JOYCE, Letter, 16 September 1904

People are never so ready to believe you as when you say things in dispraise of yourself; and you are never so much amazed as when they take you at your word.

SOMERSET MAUGHAM, Attrib.

What we have loved,
Others will love, and we will teach them how;
Instruct them how the mind of man becomes
A thousand times more beautiful than the earth
On which he dwells.
WILLIAM WORDSWORTH, 'The Prelude'

Duty ... most barren of all bonds between man and man.
OSCAR WILDE, *De Profundis*

Almost all laboured under one or other of these
disqualifications for being agreeable –
Want of sense, either natural or improved
– want of elegance – want of spirits – or want of temper.
JANE AUSTEN, *Sense and Sensibility*

Jealous souls ... are not ever jealous for the cause,
But jealous for they're jealous. It is a monster
Begot upon itself, born of itself.
WILLIAM SHAKESPEARE, *Othello*

For thus the royal mandate ran,
When first the human race began;
'The social, friendly, honest man,
Whate'er he be –
`Tis *he* fulfils great Nature's plan,
And none but he.'
ROBERT BURNS, 'Second Epistle to J. Lapraik'

There is always something in our enemy that we like, and something in our sweetheart that we dislike. It is this entanglement of moods which makes us old, and puckers our brows and deepens the furrows about our eyes.

W. B. YEATS, *The Celtic Twilight*

We may almost say that a man is only as strong as his weakest moment.

ANTHONY TROLLOPE, *Ralph the Heir*

Documents … are the wordly resources of suspicious people.

LORD BYRON, Letter to Lady Byron, 1821

The public responds now only to an appeal to its vices.

D. H. LAWRENCE, *Lady Chatterley's Lover*

Men hate more steadily than they love.

DR JOHNSON, Attrib.

I will put down a simile of human life as far as I now perceive it … I compare human life to a large Mansion of Many Apartments, two of which I can only describe, the doors of the rest being as yet shut upon me.

JOHN KEATS, Letter to J. H. Reynolds, May 1818

From the foldings of its robe, [the Spirit] brought two
children; wretched, abject, frightful, hideous, miserable. ...
'This boy is Ignorance. This girl is Want. Beware them both
... but most of all beware this boy, for on his brow I see that
written which is Doom.'
CHARLES DICKENS, *A Christmas Carol*

I loathe saving. It turns human nature sour.
GEORGE BERNARD SHAW, *Village Wooing*

Sighs will ever trouble human breath.
WILLIAM WORDSWORTH, 'An Evening Walk'

It is strange that we who are capable of so much suffering,
should inflict so much suffering.
VIRGINIA WOOLF, *The Waves*

There is a wonderful callousness in human nature which
enables us to live.
ROBERT LOUIS STEVENSON, Letter to Edmund Gosse, October 1879

In spite of his fine theoretic positions,
Mankind is a science defies definitions.
ROBERT BURNS, 'Sketch in Verse'

Those, who have never felt the anxiety, cannot fully realize
the relief.
LEWIS CARROLL, *Three Years in a Curatorship*

[143]

If you pick up a starving dog and make him prosperous, he will not bite you. This is the principal difference between a dog and a man.

MARK TWAIN, *Pudd'nhead Wilson*

I'll give you my opinion of the human race in a nutshell ... Their heart's in the right place, but their head is a thoroughly inefficient organ.

SOMERSET MAUGHAM, Attrib.

There is an electric fire in human nature tending to purify – so that among these human creatures there is continually some birth of new heroism. The pity is that we must wonder at it; as we should at finding a pearl in rubbish.

JOHN KEATS, Letter to George and Georgiana Keats, March 1818

Who can be wise, amazed, temperate, and furious, Loyal and neutral, in a moment? – No man.

WILLIAM SHAKESPEARE, *Macbeth*

Human nature at bottom is romantic rather than ascetic.

THOMAS HARDY, *The Return of the Native*

The man whose sympathies have been deadened, and whose selfishness has been fostered, by the contemplation of pain deliberately inflicted, may be the parents of others equally brutalized, and so bequeath a curse to future ages.

LEWIS CARROLL, *Popular Fallacies about Vivisection*

The difference, he observed, between a well-bred and an
ill-bred man is this: 'One immediately attracts your liking,
the other your aversion. You love the one till you find reason
to hate him; you hate the other
till you find reason to love him.'
Dr Johnson, Attrib.

FOOD AND DRINK

I'm only a beer teetotaller, not a champagne teetotaller.
GEORGE BERNARD SHAW, *Candida*

Strong ale was ablution,
Small beer persecution,
A dram was momento mori;
But a full-flowing bowl
Was the saving his soul,
And port was celestial glory.
ROBERT BURNS, 'Epitaph on John Dove, Innkeeper'

Hunger never saw bad bread.
BENJAMIN FRANKLIN, *Poor Richard's Almanack*

We do not recommend the practice of eating cheese with a knife and fork in one hand, and a spoon and wine-glass in the other; there is a kind of awkwardness in the action which no amount of practice can entirely dispel.
LEWIS CARROLL, *Through the Looking-Glass*

I never yet knew the man who said he had ate enough asparagus.
SYDNEY SMITH, Attrib.

Good wine is a good familiar creature if it be well used.
WILLIAM SHAKESPEARE, *Othello*

The heavy port drinker must be prepared to make some
sacrifice of personal beauty and agility.
EVELYN WAUGH, *Wine in Peace and War*

[On being served a disappointing wartime meal]
I think a grave has walked over my goose.
NOËL COWARD, Attrib.

[On being warned by her doctor that if she didn't stop
drinking she would be dead within a month]
'Promises, promises!'
DOROTHY PARKER, Attrib.

A good eater must be a good man; for a good eater must have
a good digestion, and a good digestion depends upon a good
conscience.
BENJAMIN DISRAELI, *Young Duke*

A nice point in human history falls to be decided by
Californian and Australian wines.
ROBERT LOUIS STEVENSON, 'Napa Wine'

Once one got the knack of it [drinking whisky] the very
repulsion from the flavour developed an attraction of its own.
WINSTON CHURCHILL, *My Early Life*

Our finer emotions should always be encouraged with a stomach moderately full.
ANTHONY TROLLOPE, *Bertrams*

Wine gave a sort of gallantry to their own failure.
F. SCOTT FITZGERALD, *The Beautiful and Damned*

Eat to please thyself, but dress to please others.
BENJAMIN FRANKLIN, *Poor Richard's Almanack*

In the matter of diet – I have been persistently strict in sticking to the things that didn't agree with me until one or the other of us got the best of it.
MARK TWAIN, *Mark Twain's Speeches*, 1910

On the whole I prefer the perfume of fruit even to that of flowers. It is more mystical and thrilling; more rapturous.
BENJAMIN DISRAELI, *Disraeli's Reminiscences*

I am convinced digestion is the great secret of life; and that character, talents, virtues, and qualities are powerfully affected by beef, mutton, pie-crust, and rich soups. I have often thought that I could feed or starve men into many virtues and vices, and affect them more powerfully with my instruments of cookery than Timotheus could do formerly with his lyre.
SYDNEY SMITH, Letter, 1837

'Tis pity wine should be so deleterious,
For tea and coffee leave us much more serious.
LORD BYRON, *Don Juan*

A man seldom thinks with more earnestness of anything than
he does of his dinner; and if he cannot get that well dressed
he should be suspected of inaccuracy of other things.
DR JOHNSON, *Johnsonian Miscellanies*

How it liberates the soul to drink a bottle of good wine daily
and sit in the sun ...
VIRGINIA WOOLF, Letter, 18 June 1939

Beware of the heresy that sherry is better for you than
cocktails. Its only medical advantage is that one drinks far
less. It is the cup that neither cheers nor inebriates.
EVELYN WAUGH, *Harper's Bazaar*, November 1933

I always did doubt a man's being a gentleman if his
palate had no acquired tastes. An unedified palate is the
irrepressible cloven hoof of the upstart.
THOMAS HARDY, *A Pair of Blue Eyes*

We dined yesterday on dirty bacon dirtier eggs and dirtier
potatoes with a slice of salmon.
JOHN KEATS, Letter to Thomas Keats, July 1818

'They have the brimstone and treacle, partly because if they hadn't something or other in the way of medicine they'd be always ailing and giving a world of trouble, and partly because it spoils their appetites and comes cheaper than breakfast and dinner.'

CHARLES DICKENS, *Nicholas Nickleby* (Mrs Squeers)

Fools make feasts and wise men eat 'em.

BENJAMIN FRANKLIN, *Poor Richard's Almanack*

'Adam and Eve were in paradise. Why? Their digestion was good. Ah! then they took liberties, ate bad fruit, things they could not digest ... Ah, to digest is to be happy.'

ANTHONY TROLLOPE, *Claverings*

Go, find an honest fellow,
Good claret set before thee,
Hold on till thou art mellow,
And then to bed in glory.

ROBERT BURNS, 'Deluded Swain, The Pleasure'

[To a lady, at dinner, who wanted action against Russia and asked him what he was waiting for]
Potatoes at this moment, Madam.

BENJAMIN DISRAELI, Attrib.

If you want to *see* a man, offer him something to eat.
It's the same with a mouse.

LEWIS CARROLL, *Sylvie and Bruno Concluded*

[On 'resting'] I could have a nice strong cocktail before dinner with a clear conscience, and no fears that it might spoil my performance. Of course it was conceivable that too strong a cocktail might spoil my performance at dinner, but I don't think it ever did ...
NOËL COWARD, *Present Indicative*

What two ideas are more inseparable than Beer and Britannia? What event more awfully important to an English colony than the erection of its first brewhouse?
SYDNEY SMITH, *Edinburgh Review*, 1823

[On being asked if she was going to join Alcoholics Anonymous]
'Certainly not. They'd want me to stop now.'
DOROTHY PARKER, Attrib.

Wine is one of the staples of civilization and, until the sinister developments of the last quarter century, was an integral part of every home with any pretension to culture.
EVELYN WAUGH, *Wine in Peace and War*

A good glass of wine is a gracious creature and reconciles poor mortality to itself, and that is what few things can do.
SIR WALTER SCOTT, *The Journal of Sir Walter Scott*

Sap will be given us for meat and dew for drink.
JOHN KEATS, Letter to J.H. Reynolds, February 1818

Eat to live, and not live to eat.
BENJAMIN FRANKLIN, *Poor Richard's Almanack*

Food fills the wame, an' keeps us livin;
Tho' life's a gift no worth receiving,
When heavy-dragged wi' pine an grieving;
But oiled by thee,
The wheels o' life gae down-hill, scrievin,
Wi' rattlin glee.
ROBERT BURNS, 'Scotch Drink'

'I rather like bad wine,' said Mr Mountchesney;
'one gets so bored with good wine.'
BENJAMIN DISRAELI, *Sybil*

First you take a drink, then the drink takes a drink,
then the drink takes you.
F. SCOTT FITZGERALD, Attrib.

White wine is like electricity. Red wine looks and tastes like a
liquefied beefsteak.
JAMES JOYCE, Attrib.

Suppose one had wine every day, at every meal –
What an enchanted world!
VIRGINIA WOOLF, Letter, 31 March 1928

One of the greatest evils of old age is the advance of
the stomach over the rest of the body. It looks like the
accumulation of thousands of dinners and luncheons. It looks
like a pregnant woman in a cloth waistcoat, and as if I were
near my time and might reasonably look for twins. I am very
glad, my dear York, that Toasted Cheese is brought in now
after dinner. I have done with fashions and look for realities.

SYDNEY SMITH, Letter, 1840

In a corner of the kitchen they found a dozen bottles bearing
the labels of various mineral waters – Evian, St Galmiet,
Vichy, Malvern – all empty. It was Mr Youkoumian's practice
to replenish them, when required, from the foetid well at the
back of the house.

EVELYN WAUGH, *Black Mischief*

Drinking may be practised with great prudence; a man who
exposes himself when he is intoxicated has not the art of
getting drunk ... he is without skill in inebriation.

DR JOHNSON, Attrib.

Englishmen, and more especially seamen, love their bellies
above anything else, and therefore it must always be
remembered in the management of the victualling of the
Navy that to make any abatement from them in quantity or
agreeableness of the victuals is to discourage and provoke
them in the tenderest point, and will sooner render them
disgusted with the King's service than any other hardship that
can be put upon them.

SAMUEL PEPYS, *Samuel Pepys's Naval Minutes*

White pudding and eggs and sausages and cups of tea. How simple and beautiful was life after all! And life lay all before him.
James Joyce, 'The Dead'

Religion

Nothing, however, can be more arrogant, though nothing is commoner than to assume that of Gods there is only one, and of religions none but the speaker's.
VIRGINIA WOOLF, *Orlando*

A veil 'twixt us and Thee, Good Lord,
A veil 'twixt us and Thee –
Lest we should hear too clear, too clear,
And unto madness see!
RUDYARD KIPLING, 'The Prayer of Miriam Cohen'

Christianity teaches us to love our neighbour as ourself;
modern society acknowledges no neighbour.
BENJAMIN DISRAELI, *Sybil*

In the English Church a man succeeds, not through his capacity for belief, but through his capacity for disbelief. Ours is the only Church where the sceptic stands at the altar, and where St Thomas is regarded as the ideal apostle.
OSCAR WILDE, *The Decay of Lying*

Heaven's best aid is wasted upon men
Who to themselves are false.
WILLIAM WORDSWORTH, 'The Prelude'

The world is in fact as silly as ever and a good competence of nonsense will always find believers. Animal magnetism, phrenology, have all had their believers and why not popery?
SIR WALTER SCOTT, *The Journal of Sir Walter Scott*

Religion is the root of all evil, or damn near all.
EZRA POUND, *Letters*

He that makes Reason his guide goes by a law of God's making, subject to no falsifications and misconstruction which all other guides whether written or others, are and must necessarily be.
SAMUEL PEPYS, Attrib.

Faith means holding the same opinions as the
person employing the word.
ROBERT LOUIS STEVENSON, Notebook

The Devil can cite Scripture for his purpose.
WILLIAM SHAKESPEARE, *The Merchant of Venice*

Don't you know, as the French say, there are three sexes –
men, women, and clergymen.
SYDNEY SMITH, *Memoir*

I told her about monasticism because we are returning to a stage when on the supernatural plane only heroic prayer can save us and when, on the natural plane, the cloister offers a saner and more civilised life than 'the world'.
EVELYN WAUGH, *Essays*

The noblest work of God? Man. Who found it out? Man.
MARK TWAIN, *Autobiography*

I consider Methodism, Dissenterism, Quakerism, and the extremes of high and low Churchism foolish, but Roman Catholicism beats them all.
CHARLOTTE BRONTË, Letter to Ellen Nussey, July 1842

Am I a mystic? – no, I am a practical man. I have seen the raising of Lazarus and the loaves and fishes and have made the usual measurements, plummet line, spirit level, and have taken the temperature by pure mathematic.
W. B. YEATS, Letter to Ethel Mannin, 1938

As I am myself partial to the roman catholic religion, it is with infinite regret that I am obliged to blame the behaviour of any member of it: yet truth being I think very excusable in an historian, I am necessitated to say that in this reign the roman catholics of England did not behave like gentlemen to the protestants. Their behaviour indeed to the Royal Family and both Houses of Parliament might justly be considered by them as very uncivil.
JANE AUSTEN, *The History of England*

I have been looking for God for 50 years, and I think that if he had existed I should have discovered him.
THOMAS HARDY, *Life*

Doesn't the Eye of Heaven mean anything to you?
Only when it winks.
NOËL COWARD, *Design for Living*

Who amongst us have not made ... some resolve ... at the
sound of the preacher's voice – and forgotten it before our
foot was well over the threshold?
ANTHONY TROLLOPE, *Bertrams*

Like all highly developed literatures, the Bible contains a great
deal of sensational fiction, imagined with intense vividness,
appealing to the most susceptible passions, and narrated with
a force which the ordinary man is quite unable to resist.
GEORGE BERNARD SHAW, Attrib.

Christ was always such a great gentleman; you can always
count on His doing the right thing ...
ROBERT LOUIS STEVENSON, *New Arabian Nights*

God knows, I'm no the thing I should be,
Nor am I even the thing I could be,
But twenty times I rather would be,
An atheist clean,
Than under gospel colours hid be,
Just for a screen.
ROBERT BURNS, 'Epistle to the Rev. John McMath'

The birth of sin was not *doing* it, but KNOWING about it.
D. H. LAWRENCE, *Studies in Classic American Literature*

Our own consciousness is incapable of having
created the universe.
EZRA POUND, *Selected Prose*

Preaching has become a byword for long and dull conversation of any kind; and whoever wishes to imply, in any piece of writing, the absence of every thing agreeable and inviting, calls it a sermon.
SYDNEY SMITH, *Memoir*

Heaven for climate; hell for society.
MARK TWAIN, *Mark Twain's Speeches*, 1910

In Ireland Catholicism is black magic.
JAMES JOYCE, Attrib.

Can you have a stronger proof of the Original Goodness there must be in this nation, than the fact that Religion has been preached to us as a commercial speculation, for a century, and we still believe in a God?
LEWIS CARROLL, *Sylvie and Bruno*

Man is a being born to believe.
BENJAMIN DISRAELI, Speech in Oxford, 25 November 1864

I believe in God who can change evil into good and I am confident that what befalls us is always ultimately for the best.
SIR WALTER SCOTT, *The Journal of Sir Walter Scott*

A Parson is a lamb in the drawing room and a lion in a Vestry
... He is continually acting. His Mind is against every Man and
every Man's mind is against him.
JOHN KEATS, Letter to George and Georgiana Keats, February 1819

I should like to see the time when Sunday might be looked
forward to, as a recognised day of relaxation and enjoyment,
and when every man might feel ... that religion is not
incompatible with rational pleasure and needful recreation.
CHARLES DICKENS, *Sunday under Three Heads*

Irreligious as I am (to your eyes) I have a devout belief
in the human soul – when I meet what can be called
such emphatically.
VIRGINIA WOOLF, Letter, 3 September 1930

I must believe in the Apostolic succession, there being no
other way of accounting for the descent of the Bishop of
Exeter from Judas Iscariot.
SYDNEY SMITH, Attrib.

Remember that the fool in the eyes of the gods and the fool in
the eyes of man are very different.
OSCAR WILDE, *De Profundis*

In the present phase of European history the essential issue
is no longer between Catholicism, on one side,
and Protestantism, on the other, but between
Christianity and Chaos.
EVELYN WAUGH, *Essays*

Ah, well, I am a great and sublime fool. But then I am God's fool, and all His work must be contemplated with respect.
MARK TWAIN, *Biography*

I am no friend to making religion appear too hard. Many good people have done harm, by giving severe notions of it.
DR JOHNSON, Attrib.

Many a long dispute among Divines may be thus abridg'd: It is so, It is not so, It is so, It is not so.
BENJAMIN FRANKLIN, *Poor Richard's Almanack*

Faith is, not to believe the Bible, but to believe in God.
ROBERT LOUIS STEVENSON, Letter to Mrs Thomas Stevenson, December 1880

As flies to wanton boys are we to the gods: They kill us for their sport.
WILLIAM SHAKESPEARE, *King Lear*

If the Jews had not prevailed upon the Romans to crucify our Lord, what would have become of the Atonement?
BENJAMIN DISRAELI, *Life of Lord George Bentinck*

If I cannot swear in heaven I shall not stay there.
MARK TWAIN, *Mark Twain's Notebook*

I believe that the reputed sinners are much more numerous than the sinners.
ANTHONY TROLLOPE, *The Small House at Allington*

Britain would miss her church, if that church fell. God save it! God also reform it!
CHARLOTTE BRONTË, *Shirley*

I think people can never have *enough* of religion, if they are to have any.
LORD BYRON, Letter to Moore, 1822

Irish Christianity is not gentle.
W. B. YEATS, *The Mandukya Upanishad*

For my part I believe that to establish the church in full power again in Europe would mean a renewal of the Inquisition.
JAMES JOYCE, *The Letters of James Joyce*, 12 August 1906

What is real piety? What is true attachment to the Church? How are these fine feelings best evinced? The answer is plain: by sending strawberries to a clergyman. Many thanks.
SYDNEY SMITH, Letter, 1834

Man proposes, but God blocks the game.
MARK TWAIN, Attrib.

Deep this truth impressed my mind –
Thro' all His work abroad,
The heart benevolent and kind
The most resembles God.
ROBERT BURNS, 'A Winter Night'

In his adventure of self-consciousness a man must come to
the limits of himself and become aware of something
beyond him.
D. H. LAWRENCE, *Pornography and Obscenity*

What the soul is to the man the Church is to the world.
BENJAMIN DISRAELI, *Lothair*

We have just enough religion to make us hate,
but not enough to make us love one another.
JONATHAN SWIFT, *Thoughts on Various Subjects*

I am a sort of collector of religions; and the curious thing is
that I find I can believe in them all.
GEORGE BERNARD SHAW, *Major Barbara*

England was Catholic for nine hundred years, then
Protestant for three hundred, then agnostic for a
century. The Catholic structure still lies lightly
buried beneath every phase of English life.
EVELYN WAUGH, *Essays*

In those days I was always in Southwark Cathedral or
somewhere hooting away 'Oh for the Wings of a Dove'.
I was always absolutely furious when I'd finished singing an
anthem absolutely beautifully to find everybody in the church
crouched on their knees and not applauding me.
NOËL COWARD, Letter to Milton Shulman, 1965

We may learn a great deal about religion,
yet not learn religion.
ROBERT LOUIS STEVENSON, 'Address to Samoan Students'

My mind rejects the whole present social order and
Christianity – home, the recognised virtues, classes of life, and
religious doctrines.
JAMES JOYCE, Letter, 29 August 1904

We cannot make laws and religions that fit because we do not
know ourselves.
VIRGINIA WOOLF, The Years

When the gods wish to punish us they answer our prayers.
OSCAR WILDE, An Ideal Husband

India has 2,000,000 gods and worships them all. In religion all
other countries are paupers; India is the only millionaire.
MARK TWAIN, Following the Equator

How slight the barriers seem to be that part Christian from
Christian, when one has to deal with the great facts of Life
and the reality of Death!
LEWIS CARROLL, *Sylvie and Bruno Concluded*

Religion is so noble and powerful a consideration, it is so
buoyant and insubmergible, that it may be made, by fanatics,
to carry with it any degree of error and of serious absurdity.
SYDNEY SMITH, *Edinburgh Review*, 1808

The only two powers that trouble the deeps are religion and
love, the others make a little trouble on the surface.
W. B. YEATS, 'A Symbolic Artist and the Coming of Symbolic Art'

Paganism never feared knowledge. It feared ignorance and
under a flood of ignorance it was driven out of its temples.
EZRA POUND, *Selected Prose*

Physicians ought not to give their judgment of religion,
for the same reason that butchers are not admitted
to be jurors upon life and death.
JONATHAN SWIFT, *Thoughts on Various Subjects*

Christianity is completed Judaism or it is nothing.
Christianity is incomprehensible without Judaism as Judaism
is incomplete without Christianity.
BENJAMIN DISRAELI, *Sybil*

In the affairs of this world, men are saved not by faith but by
the want of it.
BENJAMIN FRANKLIN, *Poor Richard's Almanack*

Who is the funny fellow who declines to go to church
Since pope and priest and parson left the poor man
in the lurch?
JAMES JOYCE, 'Dooleysprudence'

Of all Nonsense, Religious Nonsense is the most nonsensical.
ROBERT BURNS, Letter to Mr Cunningham, 10 September 1792

Serving God is doing Good to Man, but Praying is thought an
easier Service, and therefore more generally chosen.
BENJAMIN FRANKLIN, *Poor Richard's Almanack*

I hate the insolence, persecution and intolerance which
so often pass under the name of religion ... but I have
an unaffected horror of irreligion and impiety, and every
principle of suspicion and fear would be excited in me by a
man who professed himself an Infidel.
SYDNEY SMITH, Letter, 1827

Hath not a Jew eyes? Hath not a Jew hands, organs,
dimensions, senses, affections, passions; fed with the same
food, hurt with the same weapons, subject to the same
diseases, healed by the same means, warmed and cooled by
the same winter and summer, as a Christian?
WILLIAM SHAKESPEARE, *The Merchant of Venice*

[169]

Men differ daily, about things which are subject to sense;
is it likely that they should agree about things invisible.
BENJAMIN FRANKLIN, *Poor Richard's Almanack*

The world has discovered by this time that
it is impossible to destroy the Jews.
BENJAMIN DISRAELI, *Life of Lord George Bentinck*

I have always striven in my writings to express veneration for
the life and lessons of Our Saviour; because I feel it.
CHARLES DICKENS, Letter to J. M. Makeham, 8 June 1870

In those holy fields
Over whose acres walked those blessed feet,
Which fourteen hundred years ago were nailed
For our advantage on the bitter cross.
WILLIAM SHAKESPEARE, *1 Henry IV*

Lord keep us from all temptation
for we cannot be our own shepherd.
SIR WALTER SCOTT, *The Journal of Sir Walter Scott*

It is agreed, in this country, that if a man can arrange his
religion so that it perfectly satisfies his conscience, it is
not incumbent on him to care whether the arrangement is
satisfactory to anyone else or not.
MARK TWAIN, *As Regards Patriotism*

'I hold another creed; which no one ever taught me, and
which I seldom mention; but in which I delight, and to which
I cling: for it extends hope to all: it makes Eternity a rest
– a mighty home, not a terror and an abyss.'
CHARLOTTE BRONTË, *Jane Eyre*, I (Helen Burns)

The man who places religion upon a false basis is the greatest
enemy to religion.
SYDNEY SMITH, *Edinburgh Review*, 1808

God was God's name just as his name was Stephen.
Dieu was the French for God and that was God's name too;
and when anyone prayed to God and said *Dieu* then God
knew at once that it was a French person that was praying.
JAMES JOYCE, *A Portrait of the Artist as a Young Man*

The days of creeds are as dead and done with
as days of Pterodactyls.
THOMAS HARDY, *Life*

The Catholic religion likes to keep on good terms
with its neighbours.
W. B. YEATS, *The Celtic Twilight*

Two great obstacles to human fraternity are religion and
nationality; of these religion is probably the worse.
EZRA POUND, *Poetry and Prose Contributions to Journals*

The Gods are dead. Perhaps they are. God knows.
ROBERT LOUIS STEVENSON, 'Light Verse'

For my part, Sir, I think all Christians, whether Papists or
Protestants, agree in the essential articles, and that their
differences are trivial, and rather political than religious.
DR JOHNSON, Attrib.

She had once been a Catholic, but discovering that priests are
infinitely more attentive when she was in process of losing
or regaining faith in Mother Church, she maintained an
enchantingly wavering attitude.
F. SCOTT FITZGERALD, *This Side of Paradise*

Is man an ape or an angel?
Now I am on the side of the angels.
BENJAMIN DISRAELI, Speech in Oxford, 25 November 1864

Catholicism is a faith which, within its structure, allows of
measureless diversity; the spacious wisdom of St Thomas
More, the anxiety about liturgical colours of the convert
spinster, the final panic of the gangster calling for the
sacraments in the condemned cell, the indignation of the
Irish priest contemplating the spread of mixed bathing in
his parish, the ingenious proofs of the Parisian aesthete that
Rimbaud was at heart a religious poet ... they are all part of
the same thing.
EVELYN WAUGH, *Robbery Under Law*

Friendship
and Relationships

If in the vale of humble life,
The victim sad of fortune's strife,
I, thro' the tender-gushing tear,
Should recognise my master dear;
If friendless, low, we meet together,
Then, sir, your hand – my friend and brother!
ROBERT BURNS, 'A Dedication'

Friendship increases by visiting Friends,
but by visiting seldom.
BENJAMIN FRANKLIN, *Poor Richard's Almanack*

The proper office of a friend is to side with you when you are in the wrong. Nearly everybody will side with you when you are in the right.
MARK TWAIN, *Mark Twain's Notebook*

Take away my love for my friends and my burning and pressing sense of the importance and lovability and curiosity of human life and I should be nothing but a membrane, a fibre, uncoloured, lifeless to be thrown away like any other excreta.
VIRGINIA WOOLF, Letter, 19 August 1930

The chain of friendship however bright does not stand the attrition of constant close contact.
SIR WALTER SCOTT, *The Journal of Sir Walter Scott*

I choose my friends for their good looks, my acquaintances for their good characters, and my enemies for their good intellects. A man cannot be too careful in the choice of his enemies.

OSCAR WILDE, *The Picture of Dorian Gray*

No man is useless while he has a friend.

ROBERT LOUIS STEVENSON, 'Lay Morals'

Be amusing. Never tell unkind stories; above all never tell long ones.

BENJAMIN DISRAELI, Attrib.

Never submit to stir a finger in any business, but that for which you were particularly hired. For example, if the groom be drunk or absent, and the butler be ordered to shut the stable door, the answer is ready, 'An please your honour, I don't understand horses.'

JONATHAN SWIFT, *Directions to Servants*

A new mistress is nothing to an old friend, the latter can't be replaced in this world, nor, I very much fear, in the next.

LORD BYRON, Letter to John Cam Hobhouse, 1814

A sound and healthy friendship is the growth of time and circumstance, it will spring up and thrive like a wildflower when these favour, and when they do not, it is in vain to look for it.

WILLIAM WORDSWORTH, *Letters*

I know three witty people all distinct in their excellence –
Rice, Reynolds and Richards. Rice is the wisest, Reynolds the
playfullest, Richards the out o' the wayest. The first makes you
laugh and think, the second makes you laugh and not think,
the third puzzles your head – I admire the first, I enjoy the
second, I stare at the third.

JOHN KEATS, Letter to Georgiana Keats, January 1820

'For what do we live, but to make sport for our neighbours,
and laugh at them in our turn?'

JANE AUSTEN, *Pride and Prejudice* (Mr Bennet)

A friend may often be found and lost, but an old friend can
never be found, and Nature has provided that he cannot be
easily lost.

DR JOHNSON, *Letters of Samuel Johnson*

[When Marlene Dietrich had been singing her own praises too
long] Cease this mental masturbation!

NOËL COWARD, Attrib.

In no condition of life can justice be more imperatively due
than from a father to his son.

ANTHONY TROLLOPE, *Duke's Children*

Laughter is not at all a bad beginning for a friendship, and it
is far the best ending for one.

OSCAR WILDE, *The Picture of Dorian Gray*

However vast may appear the world in which we move,
we all of us live in a limited circle.
BENJAMIN DISRAELI, *Endymion*

I have ever found that those I liked longest and best,
I took to at first sight.
LORD BYRON, Letter to Moore, 1823

Do not do unto others as you would that they should do unto
you. Their tastes may not be the same.
GEORGE BERNARD SHAW, *Maxims for Revolutionists*

That is just the way in this world; an enemy can partly ruin
a man, but it takes a good-natured injudicious friend to
complete the thing and make it perfect.
MARK TWAIN, *Pudd'nhead Wilson*

I am either too self-centred, or too diffident, or too reserved,
or too shy to be able to be on confidential terms with anyone
I know at all well.
SOMERSET MAUGHAM, Attrib.

A friend should bear his friend's infirmities.
WILLIAM SHAKESPEARE, *Julius Caesar*

A wet Sunday evening – the very time of all others when if a
friend is at hand the heart must be opened.
JANE AUSTEN, *Mansfield Park*, III

If to love thy heart denies,
Oh, in pity hide the sentence
Under friendship's kind disguise!
ROBERT BURNS, 'Thou Fair Eliza'

Friendship is certainly the finest balm for the pangs of
disappointed love.
JANE AUSTEN, *Northanger Abbey*

Love your neighbour, but don't pull down your hedge.
BENJAMIN FRANKLIN, *Poor Richard's Almanack*

The powers and the grounds of friendship are a mystery.
ROBERT LOUIS STEVENSON, 'Old Mortality'

Between metaphysics, mountains, lakes, love
unextinguishable, thoughts unutterable, and the nightmare
of my own delinquencies, I should, many a good day, have
blown my brains out, but for the recollection that it would
have given pleasure to my mother-in-law.
LORD BYRON, Letter to Moore, 1817

I know people of all kinds, from the great to the little.
They don't have to wear coronets to fascinate me.
NOËL COWARD, *Daily Mail*, 1959

I do not incline to make what is called literary acquaintances.
SIR WALTER SCOTT, *The Journal of Sir Walter Scott*

Why is it that relations between different people were so unsatisfactory, so fragmentary, so hazardous and words so dangerous that the instinct to sympathise with another human being was an instinct to be examined carefully and probably crushed.

VIRGINIA WOOLF, *The Voyage Out*

A few yards in London dissolve or cement friendship.

SYDNEY SMITH, Attrib.

If a man does not make new acquaintance as he advances through life, he will soon find himself left alone.
A man, Sir, should keep his friendship *in constant repair*.

DR JOHNSON, Attrib.

Thank God there are many who will sacrifice their worldly interest for a friend: I wish there were more who would sacrifice their passions.

JOHN KEATS, Letter to Georgiana Keats, January 1820

There are few reflexions more pleasing than the consciousness, that one has contributed in the smallest degree to diminish the anxiety of one's friends.

WILLIAM WORDSWORTH, *Letters*

It is very well to have friends to lean upon, but it is not always well to lean upon one's friends.

ANTHONY TROLLOPE, *Orley Farm*

'Business, you know, may bring money, but friendship hardly ever does.'
JANE AUSTEN, *Emma* (John Knightley)

Parentage is a very important profession, but no test of fitness for it is ever imposed in the interest of the children.
GEORGE BERNARD SHAW, *Everybody's Political What's What*

Every time you force your feelings, you damage yourself and produce the opposite effect to the one you want. Try to force yourself to love somebody, and you are bound to end by detesting that same somebody.
D. H. LAWRENCE, *Nobody Loves Me*

The holy passion of Friendship is of so sweet and steady and loyal and enduring a nature that it will last through a whole lifetime, if not asked to lend money.
MARK TWAIN, *Pudd'nhead Wilson*

O that I had Orpheus lute – and was able to charm away all your Griefs and Cares – but all my power is a Mite – amid all your troubles I shall ever be your sincere and affectionate friend …
JOHN KEATS, Letter to Benjamin Bailey, 3 November 1817

My idea of an agreeable person is a person who agrees with me.
BENJAMIN DISRAELI, *Lothair*

If it be possible, never tell a lie to your master or lady, unless you have some hopes that they cannot find it out in less than half an hour.
JONATHAN SWIFT, *Directions to Servants*

Talk is indeed both the scene and instrument of friendship.
ROBERT LOUIS STEVENSON, 'The Day After Tomorrow'

Unbidden guests
Are often welcomest when they are gone.
WILLIAM SHAKESPEARE, *1 Henry VI*

That he's the poor man's friend in need,
The gentleman in word and deed,
It's not thro' terror of damnation,
It's just a carnal inclination.
ROBERT BURNS, 'A Dedication'

'To find a man agreeable whom one is determined to hate! –
Do not wish me such an evil.'
JANE AUSTEN, *Pride and Prejudice* (Elizabeth Bennet)

Hear no ill of a Friend, nor speak any of an Enemy.
BENJAMIN FRANKLIN, *Poor Richard's Almanack*

I don't believe I have any enemies ... A few teeth-grinders in the background, perhaps, but no outward enemies.
NOËL COWARD, *Daily Mail*, 1966

I have always felt the value of having access to persons of
talent and genius to be the best part of a
literary man's prerogative.
SIR WALTER SCOTT, *The Letters of Sir Walter Scott*

—

You have no one in the world besides me who would sacrifice
anything for you – I feel myself the only Protector you have.
JOHN KEATS, Letter to Fanny Keats, February 1819

—

That lust for duelling of which you used to accuse me ... has
long subsided into a moderate desire of killing one's more
personal enemies.
LORD BYRON, Letter to Hobhouse, 1819

—

One rank's as well's another ...
For he but meets a brother.
ROBERT BURNS, 'Lines on Meeting with Lord Daer'

—

It's very hard to make friends. It requires that one should give
all oneself without a thought of return.
SOMERSET MAUGHAM, Attrib.

Money and Work

'Annual income twenty pounds, annual expenditure nineteen nineteen six, result happiness. Annual income twenty pounds, annual expenditure twenty pounds ought and six, result misery.'
CHARLES DICKENS, *David Copperfield* (Mr Micawber)

Nothing but money is sweeter than honey.
BENJAMIN FRANKLIN, *Poor Richard's Almanack*

No man will take counsel, but every man will take money: therefore money is better than counsel.
JONATHAN SWIFT, *Thoughts on Various Subjects*

No! It is not money that is the root of the evil. The root is greed, the lust for monopoly.
EZRA POUND, *Selected Prose*

For my becoming your security in matter of money is a thing I have never given way to, on behalf of my owne Brother, and therefore must entreate your excuseing my not doing it in any other's case.
SAMUEL PEPYS, Attrib.

Man is an idle animal.
ROBERT LOUIS STEVENSON, 'The Day After Tomorrow'

It is no use doing what you like; you have to like what you do
... human beings may be divided into three classes; those who
are toiled to death, those who are worried to death, and those
who are bored to death.

Winston Churchill, *Thoughts and Adventures*

The idea that to make a man work you've got to hold gold in
front of his eyes is a growth, not an axiom. We've done that
for so long that we've forgotten there's any other way.

F. Scott Fitzgerald, *This Side of Paradise*

Gold! yellow, glittering, precious gold ...
Thus much of this will make black gold, foul fair,
Wrong right, base noble, old young, coward valiant,
This yellow slave
Will knit and break religions ... place thieves
And give them title, knee and approbation
With senators on the bench.

William Shakespeare, *Timon of Athens*

'People always live for ever when there is any
annuity to be paid them.'

Jane Austen, *Sense and Sensibility*, I (Mrs John Dashwood)

Money and time are the heaviest burdens of life, and the
unhappiest of mortals are those who have more of either than
they know how to use.

Dr Johnson, *The Idler*

I have sometimes envied rich citizens but it was a mean and erroneous feeling ... Better be a poor gentleman after all.
SIR WALTER SCOTT, *The Journal of Sir Walter Scott*

As a general rule no one has money who ought to have it.
BENJAMIN DISRAELI, *Endymion*

I don't know why they [Marxist critics] attack me. Nobody in any of my books is worth more than a thousand pounds.
JAMES JOYCE, Attrib.

The saddest object in civilisation, and to my mind the greatest confession of its failure, is the man who can work, who wants to work, and who is not allowed to work.
ROBERT LOUIS STEVENSON, Attrib.

There is only one class nowadays: moneyboys. The moneyboy and the moneygirl, the only difference is how much you've got, and how much you want.
D. H. LAWRENCE, *Lady Chatterley's Lover*

Simple rules for saving money: To save half, when you are fired by an eager impulse to contribute to a charity, wait, and count forty. To save three-quarters, count sixty. To save it all, count sixty-five.
MARK TWAIN, *Following the Equator*

Poverty is no disgrace to a man, but it is
confoundedly inconvenient.
SYDNEY SMITH, Attrib.

The only way to enjoy life is to work.
Work is much more fun than fun.
NOËL COWARD, Attrib.

There is hardly a pleasure in life equal to that of laying out
money with a conviction that it will come back again.
The conviction, alas, is so often ill founded, but the pleasure
is the same.
ANTHONY TROLLOPE, *Ralph the Heir*

The seamen are the most adventurous creatures in the world,
and the most free of their money after all their dangers
when they come to receive it.
SAMUEL PEPYS, *Samuel Pepys's Naval Minutes*

I know, not from theory but from practice, that you can live
infinitely better with a very little money and a lot of spare
time, than with more money and less time. Time is not
money, but it is almost everything else.
EZRA POUND, *Selected Prose*

He does not possess wealth; it possesses him.
BENJAMIN FRANKLIN, *Poor Richard's Almanack*

Money is indeed the most important thing in the world;
and all sound and successful personal and national morality
should have this fact for its basis.
GEORGE BERNARD SHAW, *The Irrational Knot*

We would all be idle if we could.
DR JOHNSON, Attrib.

The warld's wealth, when I think on,
Its pride and the lave o't;
My curse on silly coward man,
That he should be the slave o't!
ROBERT BURNS, 'Poortith Cauld and Restless Love'

Life is a pill which none of us can bear to swallow without
gilding; yet for the poor we delight in stripping it still bearer,
and are not ashamed to show even visible displeasure if ever
the bitter taste is taken from their mouths.
DR JOHNSON, *Johnsonian Miscellanies*

Nowadays we are all of us so hard up, that the
only pleasant things to pay are compliments.
They're the only thing we can pay.
OSCAR WILDE, *Lady Windermere's Fan*

Wealth is only useful for two things:
a yacht and a string quartette.
ROBERT LOUIS STEVENSON, Letter to R. A. M. Stevenson, October 1887

Saving is a very fine thing.
Especially when your parents have done it for you.
WINSTON CHURCHILL, Attrib.

If you would know the value of Money, go and borrow some.
BENJAMIN FRANKLIN, *Poor Richard's Almanack*

Sure, you make money writing on the coast, and God knows
you earn it, but that money is like so much compressed snow.
It goes so fast it melts in your hand.
DOROTHY PARKER, Attrib.

'A narrow income has a tendency to contract the mind,
and sour the temper.'
JANE AUSTEN, *Emma* (Emma Woodhouse)

Misunderstandings about money have been,
and continue to be, intentional.
EZRA POUND, *Selected Prose*

It is as good as earning money, to have very small expenses.
D. H. LAWRENCE, Letter to Martin Secker, 1926

It is essentially cleaner to be corrupt and rich than it is to be
innocent and poor.
F. SCOTT FITZGERALD, *This Side of Paradise*

There is an old time toast which is golden for its beauty.
'When you ascend the hill of prosperity may you not meet a
friend.'
MARK TWAIN, *Following the Equator*

When a man pretends love, but courts for money, he is like
a juggler, who conjures away your shilling, and conveys
something very indecent under the hat.
JONATHAN SWIFT, *Thoughts on Various Subjects*

I don't know what liberty means, – never having seen it, – but
wealth is power all over the world; and as a shilling performs
the duty of a pound (besides sun and sky and beauty for
nothing) in the East, – *that* is the country.
LORD BYRON, *Journal*, 1813

Neither trust, nor contend, nor lay wagers, nor lend;
And you'll have peace to your life's end.
BENJAMIN FRANKLIN, *Poor Richard's Almanack*

Praise [and] money, the two corrupters of mankind.
DR JOHNSON, Attrib.

It will be very hard to persuade me that anyone has earned an
income of a hundred thousand.
ROBERT LOUIS STEVENSON, 'Lay Morals'

Debt is the prolific mother of folly and crime.
BENJAMIN DISRAELI, *Henrietta Temple*

One must destroy the spirit of money, the blind spirit of
possession ... The only permanent thing is *consummation* in
love or hate.
D. H. Lawrence, Letter to Lady Cynthia Asquith, 1915

The wealthiest man among us is the best:
No grandeur now in nature or in book
Delights us.
William Wordsworth, 'Lines Written in Early Spring'

To enjoy leisure, it is absolutely necessary it
should be preceded by occupation.
Sir Walter Scott, *Monastery*

Office-hours – which I suppose reduce most men to the
condition of a coffee-mill or a mangle.
Lewis Carroll, *Sylvie and Bruno Concluded*

There is one piece of advice, in a life of study, which I think
no one will object to: that is, every now and then, to be
completely idle, to do nothing at all.
Sydney Smith, *Sketches of Moral Philosophy*

My generation of radicals and breakers-down never found
anything to take the place of the old virtues of work and
courage and the old graces of courtesy and politeness.
F. Scott Fitzgerald, *The Letters*, July 1938

'If [money's] a good thing, and can do anything ... I wonder why it didn't save me my mama.'
CHARLES DICKENS, *Dombey and Son* (Paul Dombey)

The question of property will never be settled till people cease to care for property. Then it will settle itself.
D. H. LAWRENCE, 'Democracy'

Wealth should not be the first object of life.
ROBERT LOUIS STEVENSON, 'Lay Morals'

For those sated readers of my work who ardently wish I would stop, the future looks dark indeed.
NOËL COWARD, *The Lyrics of Noel Coward*

Money and good Manners make the Gentleman.
BENJAMIN FRANKLIN, *Poor Richard's Almanack*

Credit is the future tense of money.
EZRA POUND, *Selected Prose*

'Be honest and poor, by all means – but I shall not envy you; I do not much think I shall even respect you. I have a much greater respect for those that are honest and rich.'
JANE AUSTEN, *Mansfield Park*, II (Mary Crawford)

The universal regard for money is the one hopeful fact in
our civilization, the one sound spot in our social conscience.
Money is the most important thing in the world.
It represents health, strength, honour, generosity, and beauty
as conspicuously as the want of it represents illness, weakness,
disgrace, meanness, and ugliness.
GEORGE BERNARD SHAW, *Major Barbara*

A man who cannot take off his hat to his work, and pay it
reverence, is not a workman in a happy frame of mind.
ANTHONY TROLLOPE, 'The Civil Service as a Profession' Lecture, 1861

If you'd lose a troublesome visitor, lend him money.
BENJAMIN FRANKLIN, *Poor Richard's Almanack*

All day at the office but a little at dinner; and there till past
12. So home to bed, pleased as I always am after I have rid a
great deal of work, it being very satisfactory to me.
SAMUEL PEPYS, *The Diary of Samuel Pepys*, 6 May 1665

The lack of money is the root of all evil.
MARK TWAIN, Attrib.

No man e'er was glorious
Who was not laborious.
BENJAMIN FRANKLIN, *Poor Richard's Almanack*

A working life is a happy one.
LEWIS CARROLL, *Life and Letters*

No man but a blockhead ever wrote except for money.
DR JOHNSON, Attrib.

Philosophy and Wisdom

O, it is excellent
To have a giant's strength, but it is tyrannous
To use it like a giant.
WILLIAM SHAKESPEARE, *Measure for Measure*

No man has ever known enough about words. The greatest teachers have been content to use a few of them justly.
EZRA POUND, *Selected Prose*

Most people are other people. Their thoughts are someone else's opinions, their life a mimicry, their passions a quotation.
OSCAR WILDE, *De Profundis*

What signifies knowing the Names, if you know not the Natures of Things?
BENJAMIN FRANKLIN, *Poor Richard's Almanack*

Every man wishes to be wise, and those who cannot be wise are almost always cunning.
DR JOHNSON, *The Idler*

It has been said that the dominant lesson of history is that mankind is unteachable.
WINSTON CHURCHILL, Speech at The General Assembly of Virginia, 8 March 1946

Truth is the most valuable thing we have. Let us economize it.
MARK TWAIN, *Following the Equator*

'Where a man does his best with only moderate powers, he will have the advantage over negligent superiority.'
JANE AUSTEN, *Emma* (Emma Woodhouse)

What we anticipate seldom occurs; what we least expected generally happens.
BENJAMIN DISRAELI, *Henrietta Temple*

Every error under the sun seems to arise from thinking you are right yourself because you are yourself, and other people wrong because they are not you.
THOMAS HARDY, *Life*

If you limit your actions in life to things that *nobody* can possible find fault with, you will not do much.
LEWIS CARROLL, *Life and Letters*

Beauty is a brief gasp between one cliché and another.
EZRA POUND, *Literary Essays*

It became high time to remember the first clause of that great discovery made by the ancient philosopher, for securing health, riches, and wisdom; the infallibility of which has been for generations verified by the enormous fortunes, constantly amassed by chimney-sweepers and other persons who get up early and go to bed betimes.
CHARLES DICKENS, *Martin Chuzzlewit*

I have been hovering for some time between an exquisite
sense of the luxurious and a love for Philosophy – were I
calculated for the former I should be glad – but as I am not I
shall turn all my soul to the latter.
JOHN KEATS, Letter to John Taylor, April 1818

When a man wants to murder a tiger, he calls it sport;
when the tiger wants to murder him, he calls it ferocity.
The distinction between crime and justice is no greater.
GEORGE BERNARD SHAW, *Maxims for Revolutionists*

There are occasions when you want a bull in a china shop.
SOMERSET MAUGHAM, Attrib.

Whenever people agree with me,
I always feel I must be wrong.
OSCAR WILDE, *Lady Windermere's Fan*

The best of luxuries, the luxury of knowledge.
SIR WALTER SCOTT, *Guy Mannering*

I take the liberty to send you two brace of grouse – curious,
because killed by a Scotch metaphysician. In other and better
language, they are mere ideas, shot by other ideas, out of a
pure intellectual notion called a gun.
SYDNEY SMITH, Letter, 1808

It is the history of our kindnesses that alone makes this world tolerable.
ROBERT LOUIS STEVENSON, Letter to Edmund Gosse, October 1879

There's a place and means for every man alive.
WILLIAM SHAKESPEARE, *All's Well That Ends Well*

The Renaissance is not a time, but a temperament.
EZRA POUND, *Spirit of Romance*

When I come upon anything – in Logic or in any other hard subject – that entirely puzzles me, I find it a capital plan to talk it over, *aloud*, even when I am all alone. One can explain things so *clearly* to one's self! And then, you know, one is so *patient* with one's self: one *never* gets irritated at one's own stupidity.
LEWIS CARROLL, *Symbolic Logic*

Three may keep a secret, if two of them are dead.
BENJAMIN FRANKLIN, *Poor Richard's Almanack*

There's only one lesson to be learned from life ... That there's no lesson to be learned from life.
F. SCOTT FITZGERALD, *The Beautiful and Damned*

Time is, after all, only the current of the soul in its flow.
D. H. LAWRENCE, *The Virgin and the Gypsy*

Nor could she help fearing, on more serious reflection, that, like many other great moralists and preachers, she had been eloquent on a point in which her own conduct would ill bear examination.

JANE AUSTEN, *Persuasion*

Reason is the stopping of the pendulum, a kind of death.

W. B. YEATS, Journal, August 1910

As for psychoanalysis, it's neither more nor less than blackmail.

JAMES JOYCE, Attrib.

It is a good thing for an uneducated man to read books of quotations.

WINSTON CHURCHILL, *My Early Life*

Never believe extraordinary characters which you hear of people. Depend upon it, Sir, they are exaggerated. You do not see one man shoot a great deal higher than the other.

DR JOHNSON, Attrib.

The well-bred contradict other people.
The wise contradict themselves.

OSCAR WILDE, *Phrases and Philosophies for the Use of the Young*

Truth is stranger than fiction – to some people, but I am measurably familiar with it. Truth is stranger than fiction, but it is because fiction is obliged to stick to possibilities; truth isn't.
MARK TWAIN, *Following the Equator*

Some men have only one book in them; others, a library.
SYDNEY SMITH, *Memoir*

Beautiful serves as a synonym for good or pretty or pleasing or nice or engaging or interesting. Beauty is none of these. It is much more. It is very rare. It is a force. It is an enravishment.
SOMERSET MAUGHAM, Attrib.

There are more things in heaven and earth ...
Than are dreamt of in your philosophy.
WILLIAM SHAKESPEARE, *Hamlet*

A slave is one who waits for someone else to free him.
EZRA POUND, *Selected Prose*

Of what use is philosophy, and I have always pretended to a little of a practical character, if it cannot teach us to do or suffer?
SIR WALTER SCOTT, *The Journal of Sir Walter Scott*

It's much harder to resist kindness than brute force.
SOMERSET MAUGHAM, Attrib.

Long and painful experience has taught me one great principle in managing business for other people, *viz.*, if you want to inspire confidence, *give plenty of statistics*. It does not matter that they should be accurate, or even intelligible, so long as there are enough of them.

LEWIS CARROLL, *Three Years in a Curatorship*

—

Those who invent vices indulge in them with more judgment and restraint than those who imitate vices invented by others.

THOMAS HARDY, *Life*

—

The stoical scheme of supplying our wants by lopping off our desires, is like cutting off our feet, when we want shoes.

JONATHAN SWIFT, *Thoughts on Various Subjects*

—

'One man's ways may be as good as another's, but we all like our own best.'

JANE AUSTEN, *Persuasion* (Admiral Croft)

—

Life [is] limited ... there are some branches of human knowledge which must be renounced by anyone who values his brain.

ANTHONY TROLLOPE, *Pall Mall Gazette*, 17 September 1880

—

Always acknowledge a fault frankly. This will throw those in authority off their guard and give you opportunity to commit more.

MARK TWAIN, Attrib.

To sum up all, be merry, I advise;
And as we're merry, may we still be wise.
ROBERT BURNS, 'Address'

To my extreme mortification I grow wiser every day.
LORD BYRON, Letter to Captain John Hay, 1819

An appeaser is one who feeds a crocodile hoping it will eat
him last.
WINSTON CHURCHILL, Speech in the House of Commons, January 1940

All crime is vulgar, just as all vulgarity is crime.
OSCAR WILDE, *The Picture of Dorian Gray*

Since every Jack became a gentleman
There's many a gentle person made a Jack.
WILLIAM SHAKESPEARE, *Richard III*

Depend upon it, Sir, when a man knows he is to be hanged in
a fortnight, it concentrates his mind wonderfully.
DR JOHNSON, Attrib.

News is what one hasn't heard.
EZRA POUND, *Selected Prose*

Uneasy lies the head that wears a crown.
WILLIAM SHAKESPEARE, *2 Henry IV*

A wonderful fact to reflect upon, that every human creature is constituted to be that profound secret and mystery to every other.

CHARLES DICKENS, *Tale of Two Cities*

Nothing should be named lest by so doing we change it.

VIRGINIA WOOLF, *The Waves*

After an age of necessity, truth, goodness, mechanism, science, democracy, abstraction, peace, comes an age of freedom, fiction, evil, kindred, art, aristocracy, particularity, war. Has our age burned to the socket?

W. B. YEATS, 'Stories of Michael Robartes and his Friends'

Truth in general must be commonplace or it would not be true.

BENJAMIN DISRAELI, *Henrietta Temple*

A true sarcasm is like a sword-stick – it appears, at first sight, to be much more innocent than it really is, till, all of a sudden, there leaps something out of it – sharp, deadly and incisive – which makes you tremble and recoil.

SYDNEY SMITH, *Sketches of Moral Philosophy*

To flatter and follow others, without being flattered and followed in turn, is but a state of half enjoyment.

JANE AUSTEN, *Persuasion*

Glass, China and Reputation are easily crack'd
And Never well mended.
BENJAMIN FRANKLIN, *Poor Richard's Almanack*

The age of the common man has taken over a nation which
owes its very existence to uncommon men.
NOËL COWARD, *The Noel Coward Diaries*, 31 December 1956

It's a poor sort of memory that only works backwards.
LEWIS CARROLL, *Through the Looking-Glass*

There is no such thing as a new idea. It is impossible.
We simply take a lot of old ideas and put them into a sort of
mental kaleidoscope. We give them a turn and they make new
and curious combinations.
MARK TWAIN, Attrib.

All great changes are simple.
EZRA POUND, *Selected Prose*

It's not the tragedies that trick us.
It's the messes. I can't stand messes.
DOROTHY PARKER, Attrib.

Was there not ignorance more than knowledge,
courage or force in our first assuming to
ourselves the Dominion of the sea?
SAMUEL PEPYS, *Samuel Pepys's Naval Minutes*

We are all in the gutter, but some of us are looking at the stars.
OSCAR WILDE, *Lady Windermere's Fan*

All great alterations in human affairs are
produced by compromise.
SYDNEY SMITH, *Edinburgh Review*, 1827

The test of a first-rate intelligence is the ability to hold two
opposed ideas in the mind at the same time, and still retain
the ability to function.
F. SCOTT FITZGERALD, *The Crack-Up*

The wiser mind
Mourns less for what age takes away
Than what it leaves behind.
WILLIAM WORDSWORTH, 'The Fountain'

Sometimes I've believed as many as six impossible things
before breakfast.
LEWIS CARROLL, *Through the Looking-Glass*

Men may make mistakes, and learn from their mistakes ...
Men may have bad luck, and their luck may change.
WINSTON CHURCHILL, Speech in the House of Commons, 2 July 1942

Sir, you talk the language of ignorance.
DR JOHNSON, Attrib.

It is very difficult for a man to believe anything hard enough for it to matter a damn *what* he believes, without causing annoyance to others.
EZRA POUND, *Letters*

One profits more by the mistake one makes off one's own bat than by doing the right thing on somebody else's advice.
SOMERSET MAUGHAM, Attrib.

The serpent hisses where the sweet bird sings.
THOMAS HARDY, *Tess of the d'Urbervilles*

You may call anything by any name without in the least changing its nature – bethinking myself that you may, if you be so minded, call a butterfly a buffalo, without advancing a hair's breadth towards making it one.
CHARLES DICKENS, Speech, 27 September 1869

Wisdom is better than Wit, and in the long run will certainly have the laugh on her side.
JANE AUSTEN, *Letters*, 18 November 1814

A bigot delights in public ridicule, for he begins to think himself a martyr.
SYDNEY SMITH, *Peter Plymley's Letters*

Knowledge of mankind is knowledge of their passions.
BENJAMIN DISRAELI, *Young Duke*

[207]

Good advice is easily followed when it jumps with our own
sentiments and inclinations.
SIR WALTER SCOTT, *Letters*

To live, to err, to fall, to triumph, to recreate life out of life!
JAMES JOYCE, *A Portrait of the Artist as a Young Man*

There is nothing either good or bad but thinking makes it so.
WILLIAM SHAKESPEARE, *Hamlet*

There is no sin except stupidity.
OSCAR WILDE, *The Critic as Artist*

It is often the case that the man who can't tell a lie thinks he
is the best judge of one.
MARK TWAIN, *Pudd'nhead Wilson*

Great beauty, great strength, and great riches are really and
truly of no great use; a right heart exceeds all.
BENJAMIN FRANKLIN, *Poor Richard's Almanack*

You won't make yourself a bit realer by crying.
LEWIS CARROLL, *Through the Looking-Glass*

Thought is not a personal possession.
It often comes of collaboration.
EZRA POUND, *Poetry and Prose Contributions to Journals*

The most unhappy hours in our lives are those in which we recollect times past to our own blushing – If we are immortal that must be Hell.
JOHN KEATS, Letter to J.H. Reynolds, 27 April 1818

Of the four great discoverers, we the last and least.
SAMUEL PEPYS, *Samuel Pepys's Naval Minutes*

A man should never be ashamed to own he has been in the wrong, which is but saying, in other words, that he is wiser today than he was yesterday.
JONATHAN SWIFT, *Thoughts on Various Subjects*

'Certainly silly things do cease to be silly if they are done by sensible people in an impudent way.'
JANE AUSTEN, *Emma* (Emma Woodhouse)

You don't want to knock a man down except to pick him up in a better frame of mind.
WINSTON CHURCHILL, Speech in New York, 25 March 1949

Sir, I have found you an argument, but I am not obliged to find you an understanding.
DR JOHNSON, Attrib.

Blessed is he who expecteth nothing, for he shall not be disappointed.
D. H. LAWRENCE, *Sea and Sardinia*

I keep six honest serving-men
(They taught me all I knew);
Their names are What and Why and When
And How and Where and Who.
RUDYARD KIPLING, 'The Elephant's Child'

Lord, what fools these mortals be!
WILLIAM SHAKESPEARE, *A Midsummer Night's Dream*

Whatever mitigates the woes, or increases the happiness of
others, this is my criterion of goodness; and whatever injures
society, or any individual in it, this is my measure of iniquity.
ROBERT BURNS, Letter to Mrs Dunlop, 21 June 1789

If you look beneath the surface of any farce you see a tragedy;
and, on the contrary, if you blind yourself to the deeper issues
of a tragedy you see a farce.
THOMAS HARDY, *Life*

Every man of ambition has to fight his century with its own
weapons. What this century worships is wealth.
The God of this century is wealth.
OSCAR WILDE, *An Ideal Husband*

Follow your inclinations with due regard to the policeman
round the corner.
SOMERSET MAUGHAM, Attrib.

When you've once said a thing, that fixes it, and you must take the consequences.
LEWIS CARROLL, *Through the Looking-Glass*

Few things are harder to put up with than the annoyance of a good example.
MARK TWAIN, *Pudd'nhead Wilson*

It is better to want what you have
than to have what you want.
SOMERSET MAUGHAM, Attrib.

From this I reach what I might call a philosophy; at any rate it is a constant idea of mine, that behind the cotton wool is hidden a pattern; that we – I mean all human beings – are connected with this; that the whole world is a work of art, that we are parts of the work of art.
VIRGINIA WOOLF, *Moments of Being*

The great thing is to know as much science as your mind will stand without turning into a man of science.
ROBERT LOUIS STEVENSON, Letter to Garrett Droppers, April 1887

It takes six to seven years to get educated in one's art, and another ten to get rid of that education.
EZRA POUND, *Literary Essays*

Nobody *naturally* likes a mind quicker than their own.
F. Scott Fitzgerald, *The Letters*, 8 August 1933

Science has driven out the legends, stories, superstitions that protected the immature and the ignorant with symbol.
W. B. Yeats, *Fighting the Waves*

I had always thought that a degree of Simplicity was an ingredient of Greatness.
Lord Byron, *Detached Thoughts*

Toleration is a great good, and a good to be imitated, come from whom it will.
Sydney Smith, *Peter Plymley's Letters*

I know of nothing that can give a better notion of infinity and eternity than being upon the sea in a little vessel without anything in sight but yourself within the whole hemisphere.
Samuel Pepys, *Tangier Papers of Samuel Pepys*

To believe in the heroic makes heroes.
Benjamin Disraeli, *Coningsby*

Civilization is a limitless multiplication of unnecessary necessities.
Mark Twain, Attrib.

'A man who has nothing to do with his own time has no conscience in his intrusion on that of others.'
JANE AUSTEN, *Sense and Sensibility*, II (Marianne Dashwood)

If our virtues
Did not go forth of us, 'twere all alike
As if we had them not.
WILLIAM SHAKESPEARE, *Measure for Measure*

In the ordinary affairs of life stupidity is much more tiresome than wickedness.
SOMERSET MAUGHAM, Attrib.

I could write a better book of cookery than has ever yet been written; it should be on philosophical principles.
DR JOHNSON, Attrib.

He that lies down with dogs shall rise up with fleas.
BENJAMIN FRANKLIN, *Poor Richard's Almanack*

I think when giving offence one should always be *dead* right, not merely defensible.
EZRA POUND, *Letters*, 1918

Love, lie and be handsome for tomorrow we die.
JAMES JOYCE, *Ulysses*

The best way of answering a bad argument is not to stop it,
but to let it go on its course till it leaps over the boundaries of
common sense.
SYDNEY SMITH, *Edinburgh Review*, 1821

The right to know is like the right to live. It is fundamental
and unconditional in its assumption that knowledge, like life,
is a desirable thing.
GEORGE BERNARD SHAW, *The Doctor's Dilemma*

Nothing is so dangerous as being too modern.
One is apt to grow old-fashioned quite suddenly.
OSCAR WILDE, *An Ideal Husband*

When all are guilty, none should play the Judge.
LEWIS CARROLL, Attrib.

Small people, casual remarks, and little things very often
shape our lives more powerfully than the deliberate, solemn
advice of great people at critical moments.
WINSTON CHURCHILL, *Thoughts and Adventures*

Cowards die many times before their deaths,
The valiant never taste of death but once.
WILLIAM SHAKESPEARE, *Julius Caesar*

A man of genius cannot help where his is born.
EZRA POUND, *Agenda*

Clothes make the man. Naked people have little or no influence in society.
MARK TWAIN, Attrib.

Wise people, when they are in the wrong, always put themselves right by finding fault with the people against whom they have sinned.
ANTHONY TROLLOPE, *Barchester Towers*

My aim is for the good of futurity,
though little deserving it of me.
SAMUEL PEPYS, *Samuel Pepys's Naval Minutes*

I have always had, and always shall have, an invincible repugnance to that mole-eyed philosophy which loves darkness, and winks and scowls in the light. I believe that Virtue shows quite as well in rags and patches as she does in purple and fine linen.
CHARLES DICKENS, Speech, 1 February 1842

I hope I am a little more of a Philosopher that I was,
consequently a little less of a versifying Pet-Lamb.
JOHN KEATS, Letter to Miss Jeffrey, June 1819

Private information is practically the source of every large modern fortune.
OSCAR WILDE, *An Ideal Husband*

Poverty wants some things, luxury many things,
avarice all things.
Benjamin Franklin, *Poor Richard's Almanack*

Laughter without a tinge of philosophy is but a sneeze of
humor. Genuine humor is replete with wisdom.
Mark Twain, Attrib.

Our history speaks of opinions and discoveries, but in ancient
times ... history spoke of commandments and revelations.
They looked as carefully and patiently towards Sinai and its
thunders as we look towards parliaments and laboratories.
W. B. Yeats, 'Magic'

Knowledge is of two kinds. We know a subject ourselves,
or we know where we can find information upon it.
Dr Johnson, Attrib.

It is necessary, in the present clash of philosophy and tyranny,
to throw away the scabbard. I know it is against fearful odds;
but the battle must be fought; and it will be eventually for the
good of mankind, whatever it may be for the individual who
risks himself.
Lord Byron, Letter to Moore, 1822

The splendid thing about Education is that everyone wants it
and, like influenza, you can give it away without losing
any of it yourself.
Evelyn Waugh, *Essays*

Passion, I see, is catching.
WILLIAM SHAKESPEARE, *Julius Caesar*

There is nothing so extravagant and irrational which some philosophers have not maintained for truth.
JONATHAN SWIFT, *Gulliver's Travels*

There are people, who the more you do for them, the less they will do for themselves.
JANE AUSTEN, *Emma*

The happiness that a generous spirit derives from the belief that it exists in others is often greater than the primary happiness itself.
THOMAS HARDY, *Desperate Remedies*

To keep industry alive there must be more industry, like a madness ... And it requires a madman to succeed in it.
D. H. LAWRENCE, *Lady Chatterley's Lover*

If a nation values anything more than its freedom, it will lose its freedom, and the irony of it is that, if it is comfort and money that if values most, it will lose that too.
SOMERSET MAUGHAM, Attrib.

Always speak the truth – think before you speak – and write it down afterwards.
LEWIS CARROLL, *Through the Looking-Glass*

We live in an age when unnecessary things are
our only necessities.
OSCAR WILDE, *The Picture of Dorian Gray*

When angry, count four; when very angry, swear.
MARK TWAIN, *Pudd'nhead Wilson*

Little Strokes fell Great Oaks.
BENJAMIN FRANKLIN, *Poor Richard's Almanack*

Patch grief with proverbs.
WILLIAM SHAKESPEARE, *Much Ado About Nothing*

Life is too short for the indulgence of animosity.
SIR WALTER SCOTT, *Letters*

I will not serve that in which I no longer believe, whether it
call itself my home, my fatherland or my church.
JAMES JOYCE, *A Portrait of the Artist as a Young Man*

If we don't know ourselves how can
we know other people ...
VIRGINIA WOOLF, *The Years*

Sir, we *know* our will is free, and *there's* an end on't.
DR JOHNSON, Attrib.

Out of intense complexities intense simplicities emerge.
WINSTON CHURCHILL, *The World Crisis*

If everybody minded their own business ... the world would
go round a deal faster than it does.
LEWIS CARROLL, *Alice in Wonderland*

A great deal of talent is lost to the world for the
want of a little courage.
SYDNEY SMITH, *Sketches of Moral Philosophy*

Premature to mention my 'philosophy', call it a disposition.
In another 30 years I may put the bits together,
but probably won't.
EZRA POUND, *Letters*

The sward is richer for the tread of a real, nervous English foot
– the eagles nest is finer for the Mountaineer has look'd into it.
JOHN KEATS, Letter to Benjamin Bailey, March 1818

There is nothing that saps one's confidence as the knowing
how to do a thing.
MARK TWAIN, *Hannibal Morning Journal*, 23 April 1910

The pith of my advice is: think what you want, the less said
the better.
F. SCOTT FITZGERALD, *The Letters*, 15 March 1940

We want incident, interest, action:
to the devil with your philosophy.
ROBERT LOUIS STEVENSON, Letter to John Meiklejohn, February 1880

In this world there are only two tragedies. One is not getting
what one wants, and the other is getting it.
OSCAR WILDE, *Lady Windermere's Fan*

A strange slavery that I stand in to beauty,
that I value nothing near it.
SAMUEL PEPYS, *The Diary of Samuel Pepys*, 6 September 1664

There was never yet philosopher
That could endure the toothache patiently.
WILLIAM SHAKESPEARE, *Much Ado About Nothing*

Be not too hasty to trust or to admire the teachers of morality:
they discourse like angels but they live like men.
DR JOHNSON, *Rasselas*

'Tis in ourselves that we are thus, or thus; our bodies are our
gardens, to which our will are gardeners.
WILLIAM SHAKESPEARE, *Othello*

Conversation and Contemporaries

Hitler ... declared that the fight was between those who have been through the Adolf Hitler schools and those who have been at Eton. Hitler has forgotten Harrow ...
WINSTON CHURCHILL, Speech in Harrow, 18 December 1940

There are amusing people who do not interest and interesting people who do not amuse.
BENJAMIN DISRAELI, *Lothair*

Dickens held it against his parents that they tried to force him into a blacking factory instead of letting him write. The last firm at which I solicited a job was engaged in the manufacture of blacking. I pleaded. If I wasn't employed I should be driven to Literature. But the Manager was relentless. It was no use my thinking of blacking. I must write a book.
EVELYN WAUGH, *Essays*

Sir, the conversation overflowed and drowned him.
DR JOHNSON, Attrib.

Only the romanticist preserves the things worth preserving.
F. SCOTT FITZGERALD, *The Beautiful and Damned*

Censure is the tax a man pays to the public for being eminent.
JONATHAN SWIFT, *Thoughts on Various Subjects*

The Idea of your sending it to Wordsworth put me out of breath – you know with what Reverence I would send my Well wishes to him.
JOHN KEATS, Letter to B. R. Haydon, November 1816

She was a great talker upon little matters.
JANE AUSTEN, *Emma*

> Goethe, an author born to arouse the
> slumbering fame of his country.
> SIR WALTER SCOTT, *Anne of Geierstein*

I was at school and college with the Archbishop of Canterbury [Howley]: fifty-three years ago he knocked me down with the chess-board for checkmating him – and now he is attempting to take away my patronage. I believe these are the only two acts of violence he ever committed in his life.
SYDNEY SMITH, *Singleton Letters*

> For years I thought my father with his experience and flair
> had discerned in me the qualities of military genius. But I was
> told later that he had only come to the conclusion that I was
> not clever enough to go to the Bar.
> WINSTON CHURCHILL, *My Early Life*

I've put in [*Ulysses*] so many enigmas and puzzles that it will keep the professors busy for centuries arguing over what I meant, and that's the only way of insuring one's immortality.
JAMES JOYCE, Attrib.

Mark Twain and I are in very much the same position. We
have to put things in such a way as to make people, who
would otherwise hang us, believe that we are joking.
GEORGE BERNARD SHAW, *Table Talk*

[On Rudyard Kipling] He is a stranger to me, but he is a most
remarkable man – and I am the other one. Between us, we
cover all knowledge; he knows all that can be known, and I
know the rest.
MARK TWAIN, *Eruption*

Questioning is not the mode of conversation
among gentlemen.
DR JOHNSON, Attrib.

Will you convey the note of thanks (enclosed) to the author
of *Scenes of Clerical Life* [George Eliot], whose two first
stories I can never say enough of, I think them so truly
admirable. But if those two volumes, or part of them,
were not written by a woman, then should I begin to believe
that I am a woman myself.
CHARLES DICKENS, Letter to J. Langford, 18 January 1858

Ulysses was a memorable catastrophe –
immense in daring, terrific in disaster.
VIRGINIA WOOLF, *The Common Reader*

A sheep in sheep's clothing.
WINSTON CHURCHILL, Attrib.

James Joyce was a writer possessed by style. His later work lost
almost all faculty of communication, so intimate, allusive
and idiosyncratic did it become, so obsessed by euphony and
nuance. But because he was obscure and can only be read
with intense intellectual effort – and therefore without easy
pleasure – he is admitted into the academic canon.
EVELYN WAUGH, *Essays*

Miss Austen being, as you say, without 'sentiment',
without *poetry*, maybe *is* sensible, real (more *real* than *true*),
but she cannot be great.
CHARLOTTE BRONTË, Letter to G.H. Lewes, 18 January 1848

Why is outlandish stuff sae meikle courted?
Does nonsense mend, like brandy, when imported?
ROBERT BURNS, 'My Peggy's Charms'

My late silence has been the muchness of my other business
and the little I have had to say to you.
SAMUEL PEPYS, Attrib.

[Judy Campbell] If you go on like that I'll throw something at you.
[Coward] You might start with my lines.
NOËL COWARD, Attrib.

Their table talk is stable talk.
BENJAMIN DISRAELI, Attrib.

I had a feeling once about Mathematics, that I saw it all.
Depth beyond Depth was revealed to me – the Byss and the
Abyss ... But it was after dinner and I let it go.
WINSTON CHURCHILL, *My Early Life*

One shouldn't talk when one is tired.
One Hamletizes, and it seems a lie.
D. H. LAWRENCE, *Women in Love*

I don't talk – I can't flatter, and won't listen,
except to a pretty or a foolish woman.
LORD BYRON, *Journal*, 1814

Lady Caroline stabbed herself at Lady Ilchester's ball for the
love of Lord Byron. What a charming thing to be a Poet.
I preached for many years in London and was rather popular,
but never heard of a Lady doing herself the smallest mischief
on my account.
SYDNEY SMITH, Letter, 1813

[Leaving her place one day at the Algonquin Round Table]
'Excuse me, I have to go to the bathroom.' (*Pause*) 'I really
have to telephone, but I'm too embarrassed to say so.'
DOROTHY PARKER, Attrib.

He [Stanley Baldwin] occasionally stumbled over the truth,
but hastily picked himself up and hurried on as if
nothing had happened.
WINSTON CHURCHILL, Attrib.

Long life to thy fame and peace to thy soul, Rob Burns. When I want to express a sentiment which I feel strongly, I find the phrase in Shakespeare or thee.
Sɪʀ Wᴀʟᴛᴇʀ Scoᴛᴛ, *The Journal of Sir Walter Scott*

How small a thing creates an immortality!
Roʙᴇʀᴛ Lᴏᴜɪs Sᴛᴇᴠᴇɴsᴏɴ, 'Coast of Fife'

The more you know, the more there is just beyond, and it keeps on coming.
F. Scoᴛᴛ Fɪᴛᴢɢᴇʀᴀʟᴅ, *The Last Tycoon*

Fortune favours the brave; and the world certainly gives the most credit to those who are able to give an unlimited credit to themselves.
Aɴᴛʜᴏɴʏ Tʀᴏʟʟᴏᴘᴇ, *Bertrams*

Oscar Wilde is to me our only thorough playwright. He plays with everything: with wit, with philosophy, with drama, with actors and audience, with the whole theatre. Such a feat scandalizes the Englishman, who can no more play with wit and philosophy than he can with a football or a cricket bat.
Gᴇᴏʀɢᴇ Bᴇʀɴᴀʀᴅ Sʜᴀw, *The Saturday Review*, 12 January 1895

In [Ibsen's] *Rosmersholm* ... there is a symbolism and a stale odour of spilt poetry.
W. B. Yᴇᴀᴛs, *The Trembling of the Veil*

There is no such thing as 'the Queen's English'. The property has gone into the hands of a joint stock company and we own the bulk of the shares.
MARK TWAIN, *Following the Equator*

[Upon attending a party given by the Prince of Wales in 1896] I realised that I must be upon my best behaviour: punctual, subdued, reserved, in short display all the qualities with which I am least endowed.
WINSTON CHURCHILL, *My Early Life*

If it is a question of talking casually in a ship or hotel with a man who wears an old school tie and one who does not, I would always choose the latter, because one can be fairly certain in advance of what the former will say.
EVELYN WAUGH, *Daily Mail*, 30 August 1930

It may be said we ought to read our contemporaries – that Wordsworth etc. should have their due from us. But, for the sake of a few fine imaginative or domestic passages, are we to be bullied into a certain Philosophy engendered in the whims of an Egoist.
JOHN KEATS, Letter to J. H. Reynolds, February 1818

There are only the pursued, the pursuing, the busy, and the tired.
F. SCOTT FITZGERALD, *The Great Gatsby*

[On *Ulysses*] It cost me nine years of my life. I was in correspondence with seven solicitors, one hundred and twenty newspapers, and several men of letters about it – all of whom, except Mr Ezra Pound, refused to aid me.
JAMES JOYCE, Letter, 8 July 1917

[On Lord Charles Beresford] He can best be described as one of those orators who, before they get up, do not know what they are going to say; when they are speaking, do not know what they are saying; and, when they have sat down, do not know what they have said.
WINSTON CHURCHILL, Speech after his appointment to the Admiralty, 1911

'I shall be sure to say three dull things as soon as ever I open my mouth, shan't I – (looking round with the most good-humoured dependence on every body's assent) – Do not you all think I shall?'
Emma could not resist.
'Ah! Ma'am, but there may be a difficulty. Pardon me – but you will be limited as to number – only three at once.'
JANE AUSTEN, *Emma* (Miss Bates and Emma Woodhouse)

[On T.S. Eliot] He is the only American I know of who has made what I can call adequate preparation for writing. He has actually trained himself *and* modernised himself *on his own*. The rest of the *promising young* have done one or the other but never both (most of the swine have done neither). It is such a comfort to meet a man and not have to tell him to wash his face, wipe his feet, and remember the date on the calendar.
EZRA POUND, *Letters*, 1914

Positiveness is a good quality for preachers and orators, because he that would obtrude his thoughts and reasons upon a multitude, will convince others the more, as he appears convinced himself.

JONATHAN SWIFT, *Thoughts on Various Subjects*

—

You call me in your speech 'my facetious friend', and I hasten to denominate you 'my solemn friend'; but you and I must not run into common-place errors; you must not think me necessarily foolish because I am facetious, nor will I consider you necessarily wise because you are grave.

SYDNEY SMITH, Letter to Bishop Blomfield, 1840

—

Why do I always fight shy of my contemporaries? What is really the woman's angle? ... Do I instinctively keep my mind from analysing which would impair its creativeness? ... No creative writer can swallow another contemporary.

VIRGINIA WOOLF, *A Writer's Diary*, 20 April 1935

—

I think to talk well is a rare gift – quite as rare as singing; and yet you expect everyone to be able to talk and very few to be able to sing.

BENJAMIN DISRAELI, Attrib.

—

[On Joseph Chamberlain] One mark of a great man is the power of making lasting impressions upon the people he meets ... He lighted beacon fires which are still burning; he sounded trumpet calls whose echoes still call stubborn soldiers to the field.

WINSTON CHURCHILL, *Great Contemporaries*

Vitality never 'takes'. You have it or you haven't it, like health or brown eyes or honour or a baritone voice.
F. SCOTT FITZGERALD, *The Crack-Up*

Randolph Churchill went into hospital to have a lung removed. It was announced that the trouble was not 'malignant'... I remarked that it was a typical triumph of modern science to find the only part of Randolph that was not malignant and remove it.
EVELYN WAUGH, *Diaries*

[To the newly married Oliviers] You can never live too well, my dears. When you live well people want to know you.
NOËL COWARD, Attrib.

Pity the best of words should be but wind!
ROBERT BURNS, 'Epistle to Robert Graham'

[On Somerset Maugham] 'That old lady is a crashing bore.'
DOROTHY PARKER, Attrib.

Mrs Gaskell's story [The Hearty John Middleton] I enclose ... I think the best thing of hers I have seen, not excepting Mary Barton – and if it had ended happily ... would have been a great success. As it is, it ... will link itself painfully, with the girl who fell down at the well, and the child who tumbled downstairs. I wish to Heaven her people would keep a little firmer on their legs!
CHARLES DICKENS, Letter to Wills, 12 December 1850

Sir, a man has no more right to *say* an uncivil thing, than to *act* one; no more right to say a rude thing to another than to knock him down.
Dr Johnson, Attrib.

I never quite despair and I read Shakespeare ...
John Keats, Letter to B. R. Haydon, May 1817

[On Stafford Cripps] There but for the grace of God goes God.
Winston Churchill, Attrib.

Posterity will do justice to that unprincipled maniac Gladstone – extraordinary mixture of envy, vindictiveness, hypocrisy and superstition; and with one commanding characteristic – whether Prime Minister or Leader of the Opposition, whether preaching, praying, speechifying or scribbling – never a gentleman.
Benjamin Disraeli, Attrib.

He seems to have read *Ulysses* from first to last without one smile. The only thing to do in such a case is to change one's drink.
James Joyce, *Letters of James Joyce*, 22 October 1932

A clean break is something you cannot come back from; that is irretrievable because it makes the past cease to exist.
F. Scott Fitzgerald, *The Crack-Up*

At his christening the fairy godparents showered on Mr
Spender all the fashionable neuroses but they quite forgot the
gift of literary skill … To see him fumbling with our rich and
delicate language is to experience all the horror of seeing a
Sèvres vase in the hands of a chimpanzee.

EVELYN WAUGH, *Essays*

Pray tell Dickens from me to remember that he is still but a
man – and that, however elated by this American Deification,
he must return to his Anthropic state, and that he will find us
(you and me) good friends but bad idolaters.

SYDNEY SMITH, Letter, 1842

Do you know who is my favourite author just now?
How are the mighty fallen! Anthony Trollope.

ROBERT LOUIS STEVENSON, Letter to Mr & Mrs Thomas Stevenson,
February 1878

[To Gertrude Stein] You were the same fine fire to everyone
who sat upon your hearth – for it was your hearth, because
you carry home with you wherever you are – a home before
which we have all always warmed ourselves.

F. SCOTT FITZGERALD, *The Letters*, 29 December 1934

I accept your obliging invitation conditionally. If I am invited
by any man of greater genius than yourself, or one
by whose works I have been more completely interested,
I will repudiate you, and dine with the more splendid
phenomenon of the two.

SYDNEY SMITH, Letter to Charles Dickens, 1842

[On Margaret Wooler] In spite of all I have gone and done in the writing line, I still retained a place in her esteem.
CHARLOTTE BRONTË, Letter to Ellen Nussey, 16 February 1850

I regard you with an indifference
closely bordering on aversion.
ROBERT LOUIS STEVENSON, *New Arabian Nights*

What a wonder we made of Sir Francis Drake's vessel, when the same voyage had been gone twice before by others!
SAMUEL PEPYS, *Samuel Pepys's Naval Minutes*

Nothing is so great an instance of ill-manners as flattery. If you flatter all the company, you please none; if you flatter only one or two, you affront the rest.
JONATHAN SWIFT, *Hints on Good Manners*

A boa constrictor, who had already covered his prey with his foul saliva and then had it suddenly wrested from his coils, would be in an amicable mood compared with Hitler.
WINSTON CHURCHILL, Speech in the House of Commons, 9 April 1941

Mr Keats, whose poetry you enquire after, appears to me what I have already said: such writing is a sort of mental masturbation - ******** his Imagination. I don't mean he is *indecent*, but viciously soliciting his own ideas into a state, which is neither poetry nor any thing else but a Bedlam vision produced by raw pork and opium.
LORD BYRON, Letter to Murray, 1820

[On Edgar Allan Poe] To me his prose is unreadable – like Jane
Austen's. No, there is a difference. I could read his prose on a
salary, but not Jane's.
MARK TWAIN, *Mark Twain's Letters*

Read again and for the third time at least Miss Austen's very
finely written novel of *Pride and Prejudice*. That young lady
had a talent for describing the involvements and feelings and
characters of ordinary life which is to me the most wonderful
I ever met with.
SIR WALTER SCOTT, *The Journal of Sir Walter Scott*

Good manners chiefly consist in action, not in words.
Modesty and humility the chief ingredients.
JONATHAN SWIFT, *Hints on Good Manners*

[Lord Northcliffe] The trouble with you, Shaw, is that you
look as if you were the famine in the land.
[Shaw] The trouble with you, Northcliffe, is that you
look as if you were the cause of it.
GEORGE BERNARD SHAW, Attrib.

[On Thomas Wolfe] He who has such infinite power of
suggestion and delicacy has absolutely no right to glut
people on whole meals of caviar.
F. SCOTT FITZGERALD, *The Letters*, 17 April 1935

[On Robert Peel] He embalmed no great political truth in immortal words. His flights were ponderous; he soared with the wing of the vulture rather than the plume of the eagle.
BENJAMIN DISRAELI, *Life of Lord George Bentinck*

My father taught me that it was flagitious to leave a letter of any kind unanswered. (Indeed his courtesy was somewhat extravagant. He would write and thank people who wrote to thank him for wedding presents and when he encountered anyone as punctilious as himself the correspondence ended only with death.)
EVELYN WAUGH, *Essays*

What is a good man,
If his chief good and market of his time
Be but to sleep and feed? A beast, no more.
WILLIAM SHAKESPEARE, *Hamlet*

[On Lenin] He alone could have led Russia into the enchanted quagmire: he alone could have found the way back to the causeway. He saw; he turned; he perished ... The Russian people were left floundering in the bog. Their worst misfortune was his birth, their next worst – his death.
WINSTON CHURCHILL, *The World Crisis*

Epstein is a great sculptor. I wish he would wash, but I believe Michel Angelo *never* did, so I suppose it is part of the tradition. Also it is nearly impossible to appear clean in London; perhaps he does remove some of the grime.
EZRA POUND, *Letters*, 1913

Thackeray may not be a painter, but he is a wizard of a draughtsman; touched with his pencil, paper lives.
CHARLOTTE BRONTË, Letter to W.S. Williams, 11 March 1848

'My idea of good company, Mr Elliot, is the company of clever, well-informed people, who have a great deal of conversation; that is what I call good company.'
'You are mistaken,' said he gently, 'that is not good company, that is the best. Good company requires only birth, education and manners, and with regard to education is not very nice.'
JANE AUSTEN, *Persuasion* (Anne Elliot and Mr Elliot)

What a man has got to say is never more than relatively important. To kill yourself like Keats, for what you've got to say, is to mix the eggshell in with the omelette.
D. H. LAWRENCE, Letter to Middleton Murry, 1926

[To someone who congratulated her with the words]
'What are you complaining about? You're married to a charming, handsome man who adores you.
What more do you want?'
'Presents.'
DOROTHY PARKER, Attrib.

The more I hear of the political, philosophical, ethical zeal and labours of the brilliant members of [Ezra] Pound's big brass band, the more I wonder why I was ever let into it.
JAMES JOYCE, Letter, 22 November 1929

You speak of Lord Byron and me – there is this great difference
between us. He describes what he sees – I describe what I
imagine. Mine is the hardest task.
JOHN KEATS, Letter to George and Georgiana Keats, September 1819

There is no limit to Macaulay's knowledge, on small subjects
as well as great – he is like a book in breeches.
SYDNEY SMITH, *Memoir*

This whipped jackal, Mussolini, is frisking up by the side of
the German tiger with yelps not only of appetite – that could
be understood – but even of triumph.
WINSTON CHURCHILL, Speech in the House of Commons, April 1941

There is in this world no real delight (excepting those of
sensuality), but exchange of ideas in conversation.
DR JOHNSON, *Johnsonian Miscellanies*

Browning made the verses
Your servant the critique.
Browning couldn't sing at all
I fancy I could speak.
Although his book was clever
(To give the deil his due)
I wasn't pleased with Browning's verse
Nor he with my review.
ROBERT LOUIS STEVENSON, 'Light Verse'

The Duke of Wellington has left to his country a greater legacy even than his fame: he has left to them the contemplation of his character.
BENJAMIN DISRAELI, Speech in the House of Commons,
15 November 1852

Charlie Chaplin is not merely unpopular in Hollywood. For many years he has been the victim of organised persecution. A community whose morals are those of caged monkeys professes to be shocked by his domestic irregularities ... Any stick is good enough to beat the man who has given more pure delight to millions than all the rest put together.
EVELYN WAUGH, *Essays*

The bond of all companionship, whether in marriage or in friendship, is conversation.
OSCAR WILDE, *De Profundis*

That wayward smooth-flowing current of chat about nothing in particular, which is perhaps the most enjoyable of all forms of conversation.
LEWIS CARROLL, *The Blank Cheque*

Of all the boring machines ever devised your regular and determined story-teller is the most peremptory and powerful in his operations.
SIR WALTER SCOTT, *Letters*

[Samuel Rogers] had produced a couplet. When our friend is delivered of a couplet, with infinite labour and pain, he takes to his bed, has straw laid down, the knocker tied up, expects his friends to call and make inquiries, and the answer at the door inevitably is, 'Mr [Rogers] and his little couplet are as well as can be expected.' When he produces an Alexandrine he keeps his bed a day longer.
SYDNEY SMITH, *Memoir*

Sir, there is nothing by which a man exasperates most people more, than by displaying a superior ability of brilliancy in conversation. They seen pleased at the time; but their envy makes them curse him at their hearts.
DR JOHNSON, Attrib.

[Bessie Braddock] 'Winston, you're drunk.'
[Churchill] 'Bessie, you're ugly. But tomorrow I shall be sober.'
WINSTON CHURCHILL, Attrib.

Men and
Women

The growing influence of women is the one reassuring thing in our political life.
OSCAR WILDE, *A Woman of No Importance*

To a woman no man is so desirable as one that a friend is in love with.
SOMERSET MAUGHAM, Attrib.

Life promises so very much to a pretty girl between the ages of sixteen and twenty-five that she never quite recovers from it.
F. SCOTT FITZGERALD, *Letters*, 16 March 1938

'I will not allow it to be more man's nature than woman's to be inconstant.'
JANE AUSTEN, *Persuasion* (Captain Harville)

What is keener than the eye of a mistrustful woman?
THOMAS HARDY, *Desperate Remedies*

It has been often enough remarked that women have a curious power of divining the characters of men, which would seem to be innate and instinctive.
CHARLES DICKENS, *Mystery of Edwin Drood*

[On Jesus] He was a bachelor and never lived with a woman. Surely living with a woman is one of the most difficult things a man has to do, and he never did it.
JAMES JOYCE, Attrib.

Literature gives women a real and proper weight in society, but then they must use it with discretion; if the stocking is *blue*, the petticoat must be *long* ... the want of this has furnished food for ridicule in all ages.

SYDNEY SMITH, *Memoir*

It's the beginning of the twentieth century and until a few years ago no woman had ever come out by herself and said things at all. There it was, going in the background, for all those thousands of years, this curious silent unrepresented life.

VIRGINIA WOOLF, *The Voyage Out*

> Do you not know that I am a woman?
> What I think I must speak.
>
> WILLIAM SHAKESPEARE, *As You Like It*

Their hearts are wild,
As the hearts of birds, till children come.

W. B. YEATS, 'The Land of Heart's Desire'

The girls of this generation have great advantages; it seems to me that they receive much encouragement in the acquisition of knowledge and the cultivation of their minds.

CHARLOTTE BRONTË, Letter to W. S. Williams, 19 March 1850

Nothing is so ignorant as a man's left hand, except a lady's watch.

MARK TWAIN, *Following the Equator*

From women's eyes this doctrine I derive:
They sparkle still the right Promethean fire,
They are the books, the arts, the academes,
That show, contain and nourish all the world.
WILLIAM SHAKESPEARE, *Love's Labour's Lost*

One should never trust a woman who tells one her real age.
A woman who would tell one that, would tell one anything.
OSCAR WILDE, *A Woman of No Importance*

She walks across in a room in such a manner that a Man is
drawn towards her with a magnetic Power. This they call
flirting! They do not know things. They do not know what a
Woman is!
JOHN KEATS, Letter to Benjamin Bailey, July 1818

Nature has given women so much power that the law has
very wisely given them little.
DR JOHNSON, *Letters of Samuel Johnson*

It is hard, if not impossible, to snub a beautiful woman – they
remain beautiful and the rebuke recoils.
WINSTON CHURCHILL, *Savrola*

A woman is only a woman, but a good Cigar is a Smoke.
RUDYARD KIPLING, 'The Betrothed'

By persistently remaining single a man converts himself into a permanent public temptation.
OSCAR WILDE, *The Importance of Being Earnest*

Woman alone can organise a drawing-room; man succeeds sometimes in a library.
BENJAMIN DISRAELI, *Coningsby*

Women are better hearers than men, to begin with; they learn, I fear, in anguish, to bear with the tedious and infantile vanity of the other sex.
ROBERT LOUIS STEVENSON, 'Talk and Talkers'

I've no doubt that if Cleopatra had been treated with valerian and massage she would never have made such a fool of herself at the Battle of Actium.
SOMERSET MAUGHAM, Attrib.

'A whole day's tête-à-tête between two women can never end without a quarrel.'
JANE AUSTEN, *Pride and Prejudice* (Caroline Bingley)

Most men and women of genius have entertained preposterous opinions.
EVELYN WAUGH, *Essays*

One realises, with horror, that the race of men is almost extinct in Europe. Only Christ-like heroes and woman-worshipping Don Juans, and rabid equality-mongrels.
D. H. LAWRENCE, *Sea and Sardinia*

The history of men's opposition to women's emancipation is more interesting perhaps than the story of that emancipation itself.
VIRGINIA WOOLF, *A Room of One's Own*

I require only three things of a man: he must be handsome, ruthless, and stupid.
DOROTHY PARKER, Attrib.

The gust o'joy, the balm of woe,
The saul o'life, the heaven below,
Is rapture-giving woman.
ROBERT BURNS, 'Epistle to Mrs Scott'

With all my presumed prejudice against your sex, or rather the perversion of manners and principle in many, which you admit in some circles, I think the worst woman that ever existed would have made a man of very passable reputation. They are all better than us, and their faults, such as they are, must originate with ourselves.
LORD BYRON, Letter to Annabella Millbanke, 1813

There's nothing shows a woman off like a good-looking man.
SOMERSET MAUGHAM, Attrib.

Remember – there's an awful disease that overtakes popular girls at 19 or 20 called emotional bankruptcy.
F. Scott Fitzgerald, *Letters*, 25 January 1940

Women are never disarmed by compliments. Men always are. That is the difference between the two sexes.
Oscar Wilde, *An Ideal Husband*

> When a man and woman die, as poets sung,
> His heart's the last part moves, – her last, the tongue.
> Benjamin Franklin, *Poor Richard's Almanack*

'A woman can never be too fine while she is all in white.'
Jane Austen, *Mansfield Park*, II (Edmund Bertram)

Men know that women are an over-match for them, and therefore they choose the weakest or most ignorant. If they did not think so, they could never be afraid of women knowing as much as themselves.
Dr Johnson, Attrib.

> To snub a petted man, and to pet a snubbed man,
> is the way to win suits of both kinds.
> Thomas Hardy, *Desperate Remedies*

No man has real success in this world unless he has got a woman to back him, and women rule society.
Oscar Wilde, *A Woman of No Importance*

The very word 'society' sets tolling in memory the dismal bells of a harsh music: shall not, shall not, shall not. You shall not learn; you shall not earn; you shall not own.
VIRGINIA WOOLF, *Three Guineas*

Heroine: girl who is perfectly charming to live with, in a book.
MARK TWAIN, Attrib.

Women accept their destiny more readily than men.
THOMAS HARDY, *A Pair of Blue Eyes*

Women ... are accustomed to look deeper into men at the first sight than other men will trouble themselves to do.
ANTHONY TROLLOPE, *Phineas Finn*

No woman can be unhappy if she eats well, sleeps well, dresses well, and she's losing weight.
SOMERSET MAUGHAM, Attrib.

As the faculty of writing has been chiefly a masculine endowment the reproach of making the world miserable has always been thrown upon the women.
DR JOHNSON, *The Rambler*

An English lady is not a slave to her appetite. That is what an English gentleman seems incapable of understanding.
GEORGE BERNARD SHAW, *Getting Married*

It is a truth universally acknowledged, that a single man in possession of a good fortune, must be in want of a wife.
JANE AUSTEN, *Pride and Prejudice*, I

I wonder men dare trust themselves with me.
WILLIAM SHAKESPEARE, *Timon of Athens*

Women it is said go mad much seldomer than men.
SIR WALTER SCOTT, *The Journal of Sir Walter Scott*

It takes a thoroughly good woman to do a thoroughly stupid thing.
OSCAR WILDE, *Lady Windermere's Fan*

Women with pasts today receive far more enthusiastic social recognition than women without pasts.
NOËL COWARD, Attrib.

'Tongue; well that's a wery good thing, when it an't a woman's.'
CHARLES DICKENS, *The Pickwick Papers* (Sam Weller)

I do think better of Womankind than to suppose they care whether Mister John Keats five feet high likes them or not.
JOHN KEATS, Letter to Benjamin Bailey, July 1818

There is a very general notion, that if you once suffer women
to eat of the tree of knowledge, the rest of the family
will very soon be reduced to the same kind of aerial and
unsatisfactory diet.
Sydney Smith, *Edinburgh Review*, 1810

'Tis woman's nature to be false except to a man and man's
nature to be true except to a woman.
Thomas Hardy, *A Laodicean*

What is a woman? I assure you, I do not know. I do not
believe that you know. I do not believe that anybody can
know until she has expressed herself in all the arts and
professions open to human skill.
Virginia Woolf, *The Death of the Moth*

What he means be brains in a woman ... is a smattering of
literary misinformation.
F. Scott Fitzgerald, *The Beautiful and Damned*

'Good-humoured, unaffected girls, will not do for a man who
has been used to sensible women.'
Jane Austen, *Mansfield Park*, III (Edmund Bertram)

There is nothing comparable to the endurance of a woman.
In military life she would tire out an army of men,
either in camp or on the march.
Mark Twain, *Autobiography*

Do you know how to tell whether a woman is any good
or not? Well, take her to a picture gallery, and explain the
pictures to her. If she breaks wind, she's all right.
JAMES JOYCE, Attrib.

The real trouble about women is that they must always go
on trying to adapt themselves to men's theories of women
... When a woman is hysterical it's because she doesn't quite
know what picture of woman to live up to.
D. H. LAWRENCE, 'Give Her a Pattern'

'I don't know what you must think of me' is what most
women say to a man when his opinion does not matter two
straws to them.
SOMERSET MAUGHAM, Attrib.

All women become like their mothers. That is their tragedy.
No man does. That is his.
OSCAR WILDE, The Importance of Being Earnest

What is prettier than an old lady – except a young lady –
when her eyes are bright, when her figure is trim and
compact, when her face is cheerful and calm, when
her dress is the dress of a china shepherdess?
CHARLES DICKENS, Mystery of Edwin Drood

A woman especially, if she have the misfortune of knowing
any thing, should conceal it as well as she can.
JANE AUSTEN, Northanger Abbey

Man is a predatory animal. The worthiest objects of his chase
are women and power. After I married Mary Anne I desisted
from the one and devoted my life to the pursuit of the other.
BENJAMIN DISRAELI, Attrib.

The billows on the ocean,
The breezes idly roaming,
The cloud's uncertain motion,
They are but types of Woman.
ROBERT BURNS, 'Deluded Swain, the Pleasure'

To begin with, ladies are cowards about
expressing their feelings before folk;
men *become* cowards in the presence of ladies.
MARK TWAIN, *Notebook*

Good name in man and woman
Is the immediate jewel of their souls.
WILLIAM SHAKESPEARE, *Othello*

Women, having all the trouble and pain of creating human
life, are less tolerant of slaughterous waste of it.
GEORGE BERNARD SHAW, *Table Talk*

These things combined with the opinion I have of the
generality of women – who appear to me as children
to whom I would rather give a Sugar Plum than my time,
form a barrier against Matrimony which I rejoice in.
JOHN KEATS, Letter to Benjamin Bailey, July 1818

It appears to me that ambition – *literary* ambition especially, is not a feeling to be cherished in the mind of a woman.
CHARLOTTE BRONTË, *The Professor*

It would be a thousand pities if women wrote like men, or lived like men or looked like men, for if two sexes are quite inadequate, considering the vastness and variety of the world, how should we manage with one only?
VIRGINIA WOOLF, *A Room of One's Own*

Women have a great advantage that they may take up with little things, without disgracing themselves: a man cannot except with fiddling. Had I learnt to fiddle, I should have done nothing else.
DR JOHNSON, Attrib.

Eve probably regained her normal sweet composure about a week after the Fall.
THOMAS HARDY, *Two on a Tower*

The woman in her maternity is the law-giver, the supreme authority. The authority of the man, in work, in public affairs, is something trivial in comparison.
D. H. LAWRENCE, *Twilight in Italy*

Ah! The strength of women comes from the fact that psychology cannot explain us. Men can be analysed, women ... merely adored.
OSCAR WILDE, *An Ideal Husband*

Often a man can play the helpless child in front of a woman, but he can almost never bring it off when he feels most like a helpless child.

F. SCOTT FITZGERALD, *Tender is the Night*

'No one can think more highly of the understanding of women than I do. In my opinion, nature has given them so much, that they never find it necessary to use more than half.'

JANE AUSTEN, *Northanger Abbey* (Henry Tilney)

The female of the species is more deadly than the male.

RUDYARD KIPLING, 'The Female of the Species'

A man thinks it quite natural that he should fall out of love with a woman, but it never strikes him for a moment that a woman can do anything so unnatural as to fall out of love with him.

SOMERSET MAUGHAM, Attrib.

The more I see of men, the less I like them. If I could but say so of women too, all would be well.

LORD BYRON, Letter to Murray, 1817

[Challenged to use the word 'horticulture' in a sentence] 'You can lead a whore to culture, but you can't make her think.'

DOROTHY PARKER, Attrib.

Men can't stand boredom as well as women.
Somerset Maugham, Attrib.

I like men who have a future, and women who have a past.
Oscar Wilde, *The Picture of Dorian Gray*

The tact of women excels the skill of men.
Anthony Trollope, *Claverings*

The test of a man or woman's breeding is
how they behave in a quarrel.
George Bernard Shaw, *The Philanderer*

In architecture, men who are clever in details are bunglers in
generalities. So it is in everything whatsoever.
Thomas Hardy, *Life*

She was not quite what you would call refined. She was not
quite what you would call unrefined. She was the kind of
person that keeps a parrot.
Mark Twain, *Following the Equator*

I don't care what anybody says it'd be much better for the
world to be governed by the women in it; you wouldn't see
women going and killing one another and slaughtering.
James Joyce, *Ulysses*

The women do this better – Edgeworth, Ferrier, Austen have all had their portraits of real society far superior to anything Man vain Man has produced of the like nature.
SIR WALTER SCOTT, *The Journal of Sir Walter Scott*

Women have served all these centuries as looking-glasses possessing the magic and delicious power of reflecting the figure of man at twice its natural size.
VIRGINIA WOOLF, *A Room of One's Own*

'There is one thing, Emma, which a man can always do, if he chuses, and that is, his duty.'
JANE AUSTEN, *Emma* (Mr Knightley)

It is easier to tell a falsehood than to pacify a discontented woman.
ROBERT LOUIS STEVENSON, 'When The Devil Was Well'

To such critics I would say, To you I am neither man nor woman – I come before you as an author only.
CHARLOTTE BRONTË, Letter to W.S. Williams, 16 August 1849

A Man's severe thinking, plus the shaking-off a cigar-ash, comes to the same total as a Woman's trivial fancies, *plus* the most elaborate embroidery.
LEWIS CARROLL, *Sylvie and Bruno*

A feminine nature, which first decides and then finds reasons for having decided.
THOMAS HARDY, *Life*

If you neglect to educate the mind of a woman, by the speculative difficulties which occur in literature, it can never be educated at all: if you do not effectually arouse it by education, it must remain forever languid. Uneducated men may escape intellectual degradation; uneducated women cannot.
SYDNEY SMITH, *Edinburgh Review*, 1810

Men are sweet and good and silly and tiresome and selfish, ingenuous and so simple. You can't help liking them.
SOMERSET MAUGHAM, Attrib.

Every man has a lurking wish to appear considerable in his native place.
DR JOHNSON, Attrib.

The fact is that men should never try to dictate to women. They never know how to do it, and when they do it, they always say something particularly foolish.
OSCAR WILDE, *The Importance of Being Earnest*

When a man is tired of life at 21 it indicates that he is rather tired of something in himself.
F. SCOTT FITZGERALD, *The Letters*, 29 November 1940

She is a woman, therefore may be wooed,
She is a woman, therefore may be won.
WILLIAM SHAKESPEARE, *Titus Andronicus*

HOPE, FORTUNE AND SUCCESS

I have never seen the Philosopher's Stone that turns lead into
Gold; but I have known the pursuit of it turn a
Man's Gold into Lead.
BENJAMIN FRANKLIN, *Poor Richard's Almanack*

'I hate the idea of one great fortune looking out for another.'
JANE AUSTEN, *Northanger Abbey* (Catherine Morland)

Hope, they say, deserts us at no period of our existence.
ROBERT LOUIS STEVENSON, *Virginibus Puerisque*

Your darkest terrors may be vain,
Your brightest hopes may fail.
ROBERT BURNS, 'Ode on the Departed Regency Bill'

Chance, Fortune, Luck, Destiny, Fate, Providence seem to
me only different ways of expressing the same thing, to wit,
that a man's own contribution to his life story is continually
dominated by an external superior power.
WINSTON CHURCHILL, *Thoughts and Adventures*

The successful man tells his son to profit by his father's good
fortune, and the failure tells *his* son to profit by his father's
mistakes.
F. SCOTT FITZGERALD, *The Beautiful and Damned*

All you need in this life is ignorance and confidence;
then success is sure.
MARK TWAIN, Attrib.

Fortune, to be sure, is a female, but not such a b**** as the rest
(always excepting your wife and my sister from such sweeping
terms); for she generally has some justice in the long run.
I have no spite against her, though between her and Nemesis
I have had some sore gauntlets to run – but then I have done
my best to deserve no better.
LORD BYRON, Letter to Moore, 1817

All you need in this life is ignorance and confidence;
then success is sure.
MARK TWAIN, Attrib.

Man is only weak through his mistrust
And want of hope.
WILLIAM WORDSWORTH, 'The Prelude'

From first to last, and in the face of smarting disillusions,
we continue to expect good fortune, better health, and better
conduct; and that so confidently, that we judge it needless to
deserve them.
ROBERT LOUIS STEVENSON, *Virginibus Puerisque*

Hope ... is of all our feelings the strongest.
ANTHONY TROLLOPE, *Duke's Children*

Success took me to her bosom like a maternal boa constrictor.
Noël Coward, Attrib.

Almost any exhibition of complete self-sufficiency draws a
stunned tribute from me.
F. Scott Fitzgerald, *The Great Gatsby*

> There are certainly not so many men of large fortune in the
> world, as there are pretty women to deserve them.
> Jane Austen, *Mansfield Park*, I

Do I seem to be seeking the good of the world? That is the
idea. It is my public attitude; privately I am merely seeking my
own profit. We all do it, but it is sound and it is virtuous, for
no public interest is anything other or nobler than a massed
accumulation of private interests.
Mark Twain, *Speeches*, 1923

You are yet too young to comprehend how much in life
depends upon manner. Whenever you see a man who is
successful in society try to discover what makes him pleasing
and if possible adopt his system.
Benjamin Disraeli, *Contarini Fleming*

It is perhaps a more fortunate destiny to have a taste for
collecting shells than to be born a millionaire ...
Robert Louis Stevenson, 'Lay Morals'

The power of fortune is confessed only by the miserable;
for the happy impute all their success to prudence or merit.
Jonathan Swift, *Thoughts on Various Subjects*

What Hope is there without a deep leaven of Fear?
Lord Byron, Diary, 1821

Most of my gift horses seemed to have had bad teeth ...
Noël Coward, *Present Indicative*

'Two nations between whom there is no intercourse and
no sympathy; who are as ignorant of each other's habits,
thoughts and feelings as if they were dwellers in different
zones or inhabitants of different planets; who are formed by a
different breeding, are fed by a different food, are ordered by
different manners, and are not governed by the same laws.'
'You speak of –' said Egremont, hesitatingly.
'THE RICH AND THE POOR.'
Benjamin Disraeli, *Sybil* (Stephen Morley and Charles Egremont)

'Depend upon it, a lucky guess is never merely luck.'
Jane Austen, *Emma* (Emma Woodhouse)

Let those who are in favour with their stars
Of public honour and proud titles boast,
Whilst I, whom fortune of such triumph bars,
Unlooked for joy in that I honour most.
William Shakespeare, Sonnet 25

Remember that when you are struggling and fighting and perhaps feeling you are getting nowhere, maybe even despairing – those are the times when you may be making slow, sure progress.

F. Scott Fitzgerald, *The Letters*, December 1938

HOME AND ABROAD

The maxim of the British people is 'Business as usual.'
WINSTON CHURCHILL, Speech in Guildhall, 9 November 1914

Our bore has travelled … You cannot name to him any little
remote town in France, Italy, Germany or Switzerland but
he knows it well; stayed there a fortnight under peculiar
circumstances.
CHARLES DICKENS, 'Our Bore'

Why, Sir, you find no man, at all intellectual, who is willing
to leave London. No, Sir, when a man is tired of London, he is
tired of life; for there is in London all that life can afford.
DR JOHNSON, Attrib.

> [A] good puzzle would be [to] cross Dublin
> without passing a pub.
> JAMES JOYCE, *Ulysses*

I did not really know where I was going, so, when anyone
asked me I said to Russia. Thus my trip started, like an
autobiography, upon a rather nicely qualified basis of
falsehood and self-glorification.
EVELYN WAUGH, *Labels: A Mediterranean Journal*

Go into Scotland again, or where you will, but begone
From this unlucky country that was made when
the Devil spat.
W. B. YEATS, 'The Green Helmet'

Assuredly Heaven did not form the Caledonian for the gay world; and his efforts at ease, grace, and gaiety resemble only the clumsy gambols of the ass in the fable.

Sir Walter Scott, *St. Ronan's Well*

There is no foreign land, it is the traveller only that is foreign, and now and again, by a flash of recollection, lights up the contrasts of the earth.

Robert Louis Stevenson, *Silverado Squatters*

Mr Silas Riley, Accountant, was a most curious animal – a long, gawky, rawboned Yorkshireman, full of the savage self-conceit that blossoms only in the best county in England.

Rudyard Kipling, *Plain Tales*

The very phrase 'foreign affairs' makes an Englishman convinced that I am about to treat of subjects with which he has no concern.

Benjamin Disraeli, Speech in Manchester, 3 April 1872

My living in Yorkshire was so far out of the way that it was actually twelve miles from a lemon.

Sydney Smith, *Memoir*

It was with deep grief that I watch the clattering down of the British Empire ... Many have defended Britain against her foes. None can defend her against herself.

Winston Churchill, Speech in the House of Commons, 6 March 1947

[267]

There are few nations, by the way, who can boast of so much
natural politeness as the Highlanders.
Sir Walter Scott, *Waverley*

We don't belong to any 'class'; we thinkers: might as well be
French or German. Yet I am English in some way.
Virginia Woolf, *Diary*, 22 September 1928

Perhaps it is necessary for me to try these places, perhaps it
is my destiny for me to know the world. It only excites the
outside of me. The inside it leaves more isolated and stoic
than ever ... It is all a form of running away from oneself and
the great problems.
D. H. Lawrence, Letter to Catherine Carswell, 1922

That most obnoxious type of countryman who
lives near a metropolis and has attained its cheap smartness
without its urbanity.
F. Scott Fitzgerald, *The Beautiful and Damned*

My heart's in the Highlands, my heart is not here,
My heart's in the Highlands, a-chasing the deer;
A-chasing the wild-deer, and following the roe,
My heart's in the Highlands wherever I go.
Robert Burns, 'My Heart's in the Highlands'

I am always sorry when any language is lost,
because languages are the pedigree of nations.
Dr Johnson, Attrib.

I have found out that there ain't no surer way to find out
whether you like people or hate them than to travel with
them.
MARK TWAIN, *Tom Sawyer Abroad*

Italian language needs sand-paper.
EZRA POUND, *Poetry and Prose Contributions to Journals*

Various Impositions we suffer'd from Boatmen, Porters etc on
both Sides the Water. I know not which are most rapacious,
the English or the French; but the latter have, with their
Knavery, the most Politeness.
BENJAMIN FRANKLIN, Letter to Polly Stevenson, 14 September 1767

This fortress built by nature for herself
Against infection and the hand of war,
This happy brees of men, this little world,
This precious stone set in the silver sea ...
This blessed plot, this earth, this realm, this England.
WILLIAM SHAKESPEARE, *Richard II*

When someone transplants himself from one country to
another he is more likely to assimilate the defects of its
inhabitants than their virtues.
SOMERSET MAUGHAM, Attrib.

It is always, I think, true to say that one of the main
foundations of the British sense of humour is understatement.
WINSTON CHURCHILL, Speech in the House of Commons, 27 July 1950

Thinking is the most unhealthy thing in the world, and people die of it just as they die of any other disease. Fortunately, in England at any rate, thought is not catching. Our splendid physique as a people is entirely due to our national stupidity.

OSCAR WILDE, *The Decay of Lying*

Anyone who has been to an English public school will always feel comparatively at home in prison.

EVELYN WAUGH, *Decline and Fall*

[Of an Irish radical] It was the battle, rather than the thing battled for, that was dear to him; the strife, rather than the result. He felt that it would be dull times in Dublin, when they should have no usurping Government to abuse, no Saxon Parliament to upbraid, no English laws to ridicule, and no Established Church to curse.

ANTHONY TROLLOPE, *Kellys & O'Kellys*

If you *unscotch* us you will find us
damned mischievous Englishmen.

SIR WALTER SCOTT, *Letters*

'We do not call Bermuda or Bahama, you know, the West Indies.'
Mrs Musgrove had not a word to say in dissent; she could not accuse herself of having ever called them any thing in the whole course of her life.

JANE AUSTEN, *Persuasion* (Mr Croft)

When shall I see Scotland again? Never shall I forget the
happy days passed there, amidst odious smells, barbarous
sounds, bad suppers, excellent hearts, and most enlightening
and cultivated understandings.
SYDNEY SMITH, *Memoir*

How sick, sick, sick I am of Dublin! It is the city of failure,
of rancour and of unhappiness. I long to be out of it.
JAMES JOYCE, *The Letters of James Joyce*, 22 August 1909

I am slowly discovering England which is the most wonderful
foreign land I have ever been in.
RUDYARD KIPLING, Letter to H. Rider Haggard, December 1902

It cannot be denied that these winter crossings are very trying
and startling; while the personal discomfort of not being able
to wash, and the miseries of getting up and going to bed,
with what small means there are all sliding, and sloping, and
slopping about, are really in their way distressing.
CHARLES DICKENS, Letter to Miss Hogarth, 16 November 1867

Like all great travellers I have seen more than I remember, and
remember more than I have seen.
BENJAMIN DISRAELI, *Vivian Grey*

Well mannered and sensible are the Southern boys. I suppose
the sun brings them forwards.
SIR WALTER SCOTT, *The Journal of Sir Walter Scott*

Americans, while willing, even eager, to be serfs, have always
been obstinate about being peasantry.
F. SCOTT FITZGERALD, *The Great Gatsby*

Go anywhere in England where there are natural, wholesome,
contented, and really nice English people, and what do
you always find? That the stables are the real centre of the
household ... There are only two classes in good society in
England: the equestrian classes and the neurotic classes.
GEORGE BERNARD SHAW, *Heartbreak House*

England's hour of weakness is Europe's hour of danger.
WINSTON CHURCHILL, *The Caged Lion*

Instead of the Liberty, Equality and Fraternity of the Americas,
Europe offers its artists Liberty, Diversity and Privacy.
Perhaps it is for this that so many of the best
American writers go abroad.
EVELYN WAUGH, *Essays*

They spelt it Vinci and pronounce it Vinchy; foreigners always
spell better than they pronounce.
MARK TWAIN, *Innocents Abroad*

It's odd how England suddenly takes shape – not that I have
any patriotic pride – only a visual lust,
and a sense of Shakespeare.
VIRGINIA WOOLF, Letter, 26 December 1936

A zealous Irishman, especially if he lives out of Ireland, spends his time in a never-ending argument about Oliver Cromwell, the Danes, the penal laws, the Rebellion of 1798, the famine, the Irish peasant, and ends by substituting a traditional casuistry for a country.

W. B. YEATS, 'J.M Synge and the Ireland of his Time

I love to go and I love to have been, but best of all I love the intervals between arrivals and departures ...

NOËL COWARD, *Present Indicative*

That dogged spirit of courage so peculiar to the English.

SIR WALTER SCOTT, *Betrothed*

I am a citizen of the world – all countries are alike to me.

LORD BYRON, Letter to Teresa Guiccioli, 1819

The Irish are a *fair people*;
they never speak well of one another.

DR JOHNSON, Attrib.

If every museum in the New World were emptied, if every famous building in the Old World were destroyed and only Venice saved, there would be enough there to fill a full lifetime with delight. Venice, with all its complexity and variety, is in itself the greatest surviving work of art in the world.

EVELYN WAUGH, *Essays*

Earth hath not anything to show more fair:
Dull would he be of soul who could pass by
A sight so touching in its majesty:
The City now doth, like a garment, wear
The beauty of the morning; silent, bare,
Ships, towers, domes, theatres, and temples lie
Open unto the fields, and to the sky;
All bright and glittering in the smokeless air.
WILLIAM WORDSWORTH, 'Composed upon Westminster Bridge'

'One has not great hopes from Birmingham. I always say there
is something direful in the sound.'
JANE AUSTEN, *Emma* (Mrs Elton)

Is it affectation or impotence of the English that they can
make no attempt to pronounce any language but their own.
JAMES JOYCE, *The Letters of James Joyce*, 13 November 1906

[On Anglo-American co-operation] If we are together
nothing is impossible, and if we are divided all will fail.
WINSTON CHURCHILL, Speech in Harvard, August 1943

The nature of the English is generally to be self-lovers, and
thinking everything of their own the best, viz., our beef,
beer, women, horses, religion, laws, etc., and from the same
principles are over-valuers of our ships.
SAMUEL PEPYS, *Samuel Pepys's Naval Minutes*

[On the French language]
It is perhaps the poorest one ever spoken since the jabbering
in the Tower of Babel ...
JOHN KEATS, Letter to Fanny Keats, September 1817

Talent is sometimes forgiven in Hollywood, genius never.
EVELYN WAUGH, *Essays*

Italy has lived more fully than other nations because she has
kept up the habit of placing statues in gardens.
EZRA POUND, Attrib.

This is a tragic city of beautiful girls – the girls who mop the
floor are beautiful, the waitresses, the shop ladies. You never
want to see any more beauty.
F. SCOTT FITZGERALD, *The Letters*, Winter 1927

'Kent, Sir – Every body knows Kent – apples, cherries, hops
and women.'
CHARLES DICKENS, *The Pickwick Papers* (Alfred Jingle)

Literature the Americans have none – no native literature,
we mean. It is all imported.
SYDNEY SMITH, *Edinburgh Review*, 1818

Am I a Free-man in England, and do I become a slave in six
hours, by crossing the Channel?
JONATHAN SWIFT, *Drapier's Letters*

I have travelled more than any one else, and I have noticed that even the angels speak English with an accent.
MARK TWAIN, *Following the Equator*

England is unrivalled for two things – sport and politics.
BENJAMIN DISRAELI, *Coningsby*

I cannot forecast to you the action of Russia. It is a riddle wrapped in a mystery inside an enigma.
WINSTON CHURCHILL, Broadcast, 1 October 1939

It has been my fate to have so close an intimacy with Ireland, that when I meet an Irishman abroad, I always recognise in him more of a kinsman than in an Englishman.
ANTHONY TROLLOPE, *North America*

They are certainly a very odd people and but for that ugly humour of murdering which is in full decline they would be the most amusing and easy to live with in the world.
SIR WALTER SCOTT, *The Letters of Sir Walter Scott*

We think you had better not leave England. Let the Portmans go to Ireland, but as you know nothing of the manners there, you had better not go there with them. You will be in danger of giving false representation.
JANE AUSTEN, *Letters*, 10 August 1814

Oh, East is East, and West is West,
and never the twain shall meet.
Till Earth and Sky stand presently
at God's great Judgment Seat;
But there is neither East nor West,
Border, nor Breed, nor Birth,
When two strong men stand face to face,
though they come from the ends of the earth!
RUDYARD KIPLING, 'The Ballad of East and West'

Travel they say improves the mind,
An irritating platitude
Which frankly, entre nous,
Is very far from true.
NOËL COWARD, *Sail Away*

Rome reminds me of a man who lives by exhibiting to
travellers his grandmother's corpse.
JAMES JOYCE, Letter, 9 October 1906

The travellers' room at the White Horse Cellar is of course
uncomfortable; it would be no travellers' room if it were not.
CHARLES DICKENS, *The Pickwick Papers*

The Americans are so like to the British, the British to the
Americans, that they have not much patience with each other
for not being in all respects the same with each other.
SIR WALTER SCOTT, *Letters*

I must learn to speak. A man must know how to speak in Ireland just as a man in old times had to carry a sword.
W. B. YEATS, *Autobiography*

The most valuable commodity for the tourist, whether he is cruising along the French Riviera in a yacht or ploughing through unmapped areas of virgin forest, is alcohol ... With a glass in his hand, the tourist can gaze out on the streets of Tangier, teeming with English governesses and retired colonels, and happily imagine himself a Marco Polo.
EVELYN WAUGH, *Essays*

As I stroll the city, oft I
Spy a building large and lofty,
Not a bow-shot from the College,
Half a globe from sense and knowledge ...
Tell us, what this pile contains?
Many a head that holds no brains.
JONATHAN SWIFT,
'A Character, Panegyric and Description of the Legion Club'

Very nice sort of place, Oxford, I should think, for people that like that sort of place.
GEORGE BERNARD SHAW, *Man and Superman*

How thankful one can be, to be out of one's country ... I am transported, the moment I set foot on a foreign shore.
I say to myself: 'Here steps a new creature into life.'
D. H. LAWRENCE, *Women in Love* (Gudrun)

Let there be sunshine on both sides of the iron curtain; and if
ever the sunshine should be equal on both sides,
the curtain will be no more.

WINSTON CHURCHILL, Speech in Blenheim, 4 August 1947

What men call gallantry, and gods adultery, is much more
common where the climate's sultry.

LORD BYRON, *Don Juan*

A map, and particularly one with blank spaces and dotted
rivers, can influence a travelmaniac as can no book
or play ... Every place in the world is worth visiting and
treasures some peculiar gift for the traveller who
goes there in decent humility.

EVELYN WAUGH, *Essays*

England is the only country which, when it enters into a
quarrel that it believes to be just never ceases its efforts till it
has achieved its aim.

BENJAMIN DISRAELI, Attrib.

France, though armed to the teeth, is pacifist to the core.

WINSTON CHURCHILL, Speech in the House of Commons,
23 November 1936

Hath Britain all the sun that shines?

WILLIAM SHAKESPEARE, *Cymbeline*

Then I shall walk, all along the Thames, in and out where I used to haunt, so through the Temple, up the Strand and out into Oxford Street ... You never shared my passion for that great city. Yet it's what in some odd corner of my dreaming mind, represents Chaucer, Shakespeare, Dickens. It's my only patriotism: save one vision, in Warwickshire one spring (May 1934) when we were driving back from Ireland and I saw a stallion being led, under the may and the beeches, along a grass ride; and I thought that is England.
VIRGINIA WOOLF, Letter, 12 January 1941

Sightseeing is the art of disappointment.
ROBERT LOUIS STEVENSON, 'The Petrified Forest'

There are no braver men than the Germans.
SIR WALTER SCOTT, *Talisman*

Even the foreigner loses his kindly politeness as soon as we get him Americanized.
MARK TWAIN, *Speeches*, 1923

Half of these Scotch and Lake troubadours, are spoilt by living in little circles and petty societies. London and the world is the only place to take the conceit out of a man.
LORD BYRON, Letter to Moore, 1814

A joke goes a great way in the country. I have known one last pretty well for seven years.
SYDNEY SMITH, *Memoir*

Venice, the eldest Child of Liberty,
She was a maiden City, bright and free.
WILLIAM WORDSWORTH, 'On the Extinction of the Venetian Republic'

It must be confessed that saving in reasonable (and therefore rare) sea-weather, the act of arrival at our French watering-place from England is difficult to be achieved with dignity.
CHARLES DICKENS, 'Our French Watering-Place'

With a common origin, a common language, a common literature, a common religion, and – common drinks, what is longer needful to the cementing of the two nations together in a permanent bond of brotherhood?
MARK TWAIN, *Mark Twain's Speeches*, 1923

England is like a woman you're desperately in love with as long as you don't see her, but when you're with her she maddens you so that you can't bear her.
SOMERSET MAUGHAM, Attrib.

What should they know of England who only England know?
RUDYARD KIPLING, 'The English Flag'

There are few virtues that the Poles do not possess – and there are few mistakes they have ever avoided.
WINSTON CHURCHILL, Speech in the House of Commons,
16 August 1945

In French you can be heroic and gallant with dignity ...
But in English you can't be heroic and gallant
without being a little absurd.

F. Scott Fitzgerald, *Tender is the Night*

This lovely land that always sent
Her writers and artists to banishment
And in a spirit of Irish fun
Betrayed her own leaders, one by one.

James Joyce, 'Gas from a Burner'

Any breath from Ireland blows pleasurably in this hateful
London where you cannot go five paces without seeing some
wretched object broken either by wealth or poverty.

W. B Yeats, Letter to Katherine Tynan, 1887

A more inefficient yet a more resolved class of men than the
Spaniards were never conceived.

Sir Walter Scott, *The Journal of Sir Walter Scott*

Nowhere, except perhaps in parts of Asia, is the class structure
as subtle and elaborate as in England. Everyone in England
has a precise and particular place in the social scale and
constantly manifests the fact in habit and word. Many writers
have found a rich source in this national idiosyncrasy.

Evelyn Waugh, *Essays*

When you tell the Irish that they are slow in recognising their
own men of genius they reply with street riots and politics.

EZRA POUND, Attrib.

Perhaps, after all, America never has been discovered ...
I myself would say that it has been merely detected.

OSCAR WILDE, *The Picture of Dorian Gray*

I have a boundless confidence in the English character; I
believe that they have more real religion, more probity, more
knowledge, and more genuine worth, than exists in the whole
world besides.

SYDNEY SMITH, *Sketches of Moral Philosophy*

For my part, I travel not to go anywhere, but to go.
I travel for travel's sake.

ROBERT LOUIS STEVENSON, 'Cheylard and Luc'

Be on your guard! I am going to speak in French – a
formidable undertaking and one which will put great
demands upon your friendship for Great Britain.

WINSTON CHURCHILL, Speech in Paris, 1944

A man who has not been in Italy, is always conscious of an
inferiority, from his not having seen what is expected a man
should see. The grand object of travelling is to see the shores
of the Mediterranean.

DR JOHNSON, Attrib.

LIFE·AND·DEATH

All women have to fight with death to keep their children.
Death, being childless, wants our children from us.
OSCAR WILDE, *A Woman of No Importance*

Death was defiance. Death was an attempt to communicate,
people feeling the impossibility of reaching the centre which,
mystically, evaded them, closeness drew apart; rapture faded;
one was alone. There was an embrace in death.
VIRGINIA WOOLF, *Mrs Dalloway*

Pity is for the living, envy is for the dead.
MARK TWAIN, *Following the Equator*

If I have given you delight
By aught that I have done,
Let me lie quiet in that night
Which shall be yours anon:
And for the little, little, span
The dead are borne in mind,
Seek not to question other than
The books I leave behind.
RUDYARD KIPLING, 'The Appeal'

Life is not designed to minister to a man's vanity.
ROBERT LOUIS STEVENSON, 'Christmas Sermon'

Promise me that my gravestone will carry only these words:
'If you can read this you've come too close.'
DOROTHY PARKER, Attrib.

Life's but a walking shadow, a poor player
That struts and frets his hour upon the stage .
And then is heard no more.
WILLIAM SHAKESPEARE, *Macbeth*

All life is revelation beginning in miracle and enthusiasm,
and dying out as it unfolds itself in what
we have mistaken for progress.
W. B. YEATS, 'The Theatre'

Life is a perpetual holiday.
WINSTON CHURCHILL, Attrib.

Those who die, and dying still can love, do not die.
They live still in the beloved
D. H. LAWRENCE, *Women in Love*

Can death be sleep, when life is but a dream
And scenes of bliss pass as a phantom by?
The transient pleasures as a vision seem,
And yet we think the greatest pain's to die.
How strange it is that man on earth should roam,
And lead a life of woe, but not forsake
His rugged path; nor dare he view alone
His future doom which is but to awake.
JOHN KEATS, *Posthumous and Fugitive Poems*

Life is a tragedy wherein we sit as spectators for a while and then act our part in it.
JONATHAN SWIFT, *Thoughts on Various Subjects*

Life is dear even to those who feel it a burden.
SIR WALTER SCOTT, *Heart of Mid-Lothian*

What a pity that in life we only get our lessons when they are of no use to us.
OSCAR WILDE, *Lady Windermere's Fan*

To believe in immortality is one thing, but it is first needful to believe in life.
ROBERT LOUIS STEVENSON, 'Old Mortality'

Somebody has said that in order to know a community, one must observe the style of its funerals and know what manner of men they bury with most ceremony.
MARK TWAIN, *Roughing It*

If there's another world, he lives in bliss;
If there is none, he made the best of this.
ROBERT BURNS, 'Epitaph on my Own Friend'

The soul is born old but grows young. That is the comedy of life. And the body is born young but grows old.
That is life's tragedy.
OSCAR WILDE, *A Woman of No Importance*

Life is beautiful, so long as it is consuming you. When it is rushing through you, destroying you, life is glorious. It is best to roar away, like a fire with a great draught, white-hot to the last bit. It's when you burn a slow fire and save fuel that life's not worth living.

D. H. LAWRENCE, *A Modern Lover*

All things have second birth;
The earthquake is not satisfied at once.

WILLIAM WORDSWORTH, 'The Prelude'

The web of our life is of a mingled yarn, good and ill together. Our virtues would be proud if our faults whipped them not; and our crimes would despair if they were not cherished by our own virtues.

WILLIAM SHAKESPEARE, *All's Well That Ends Well*

Dead! says Alf. He's no more dead than you are. Maybe so, says Joe. They took the liberty of burying him this morning anyhow.

JAMES JOYCE, *Ulysses*

A just conception of life is too large a thing to grasp during the short interval of passing through it.

THOMAS HARDY, *A Pair of Blue Eyes*

Why is life so tragic; so like a strip of pavement over an abyss.

VIRGINIA WOOLF, *Diary*, 25 October 1920

There is only one wish realisable on the earth; only one thing
that can be perfectly attained: Death. And from a variety
of circumstances we have no one to tell us whether it be
worth attaining.

ROBERT LOUIS STEVENSON, 'El Dorado'

There's little in taking or giving
There's little in water or wine;
This living, this living, this living
Was never a project of mine.

DOROTHY PARKER, 'Coda'

I cannot but return my sincere thanks to the high gods for the
gift of existence. All the days were good and each day better
than the other. Ups and downs, risks and journeys, but
always the sense of motion, and the illusion of hope.

WINSTON CHURCHILL, *My Early Life*

Death must be distinguished from dying,
with which it is often confounded.

SYDNEY SMITH, *Memoir*

I emphatically direct that I be buried in an inexpensive,
unostentatious, and strictly private manner ... and that those
who attend my funeral wear no scarf, cloak, black bow, long-
hatband, or other such revolting absurdity.

CHARLES DICKENS, Dickens's Will

Whoever has lived long enough to find out what life is, knows how deep a debt of gratitude we owe to Adam, the first great benefactor of our race. He brought death into the world.
MARK TWAIN, *Pudd'nhead Wilson*

To be entirely free, and at the same time entirely dominated by law, is the eternal paradox of human life.
OSCAR WILDE, *De Profundis*

We have given the world our passion,
We have naught for death but toys.
W. B. YEATS, 'Upon a Dying Lady'

I have no fear of death itself, but only the long wait for it. When once a man has made up his mind that God means to do him good, he ceases to fear death.
ANTHONY TROLLOPE, *Guardian*, 11 December 1882

Life levels all men: death reveals the eminent.
GEORGE BERNARD SHAW, *Maxims for Revolutionists*

It seems to me most strange that men should fear,
Seeing that death, a necessary end,
Will come when it will come.
WILLIAM SHAKESPEARE, *Julius Caesar*

Life is a Permanent Possibility of Sensation.
ROBERT LOUIS STEVENSON, 'El Dorado'

I could not look on Death, which being known,
Men led me to him, blindfold and alone.
RUDYARD KIPLING, 'The Coward'

When Death's pale horse runs away with persons on full
speed, an active physician may possibly give them a turn;
but if he carries them on an even slow pace, down hill too!
no care nor skill can save them!
DR JOHNSON, *Johnsonian Miscellanies*

When one subtracts from life infancy (which is vegetation)
– sleep, eating, and swilling – buttoning and unbuttoning –
how much remains of downright existence?
The summer of a dormouse.
LORD BYRON, *Journal*, 1813

Every love's the love before
In a duller dress.
That's the measure of my lore –
Here's my bitterness:
Would I knew a little more,
Or very much less!
DOROTHY PARKER, 'Summary'

The strange thing about life is that though the nature of it
must have been apparent to every one for hundreds of years,
no one has left any adequate account of it.
VIRGINIA WOOLF, *Jacob's Room*

No preacher is listened to but Time, which gives us the same train and turn of thought that elder people have in vain tried to put into our heads before.
JONATHAN SWIFT, *Thoughts on Various Subjects*

Life is terrible. It rules us, we do not rule it.
OSCAR WILDE, *Lady Windermere's Fan*

And come he slow, or come he fast,
It is but Death who comes at last.
SIR WALTER SCOTT, *Marmion*

Let us endeavour so to live that when we come to die
even the undertaker will be sorry.
MARK TWAIN, *Pudd'nhead Wilson*

Life is but a day at most,
Sprung from night, in darkness lost;
Hope not sunshine every hour,
Fear not clouds will always lour.
ROBERT BURNS, 'Written in Friars' Carse Hermitage'

When we are born we cry, that we are come
To this great stage of fools.
WILLIAM SHAKESPEARE, *King Lear*

Time's winged chariot seems to be goosing me.
NOËL COWARD, *The Noel Coward Diaries*, 1959

One by one they were all becoming shades. Better pass boldly into that other world, in the full glory of some passion, than fade and wither dismally with age.
JAMES JOYCE, 'The Dead'

Cease to live I may; but not cease to be: it can only be a change of function.
ROBERT LOUIS STEVENSON, Notebook

We have buried our dead out of our sight.
CHARLOTTE BRONTË, Letter to W. S. Williams, 2 October 1848

We begin to live when we conceive life as tragedy.
W. B. YEATS, *The Trembling of the Veil*

One can survive anything nowadays, except death, and live down anything except a good reputation.
OSCAR WILDE, *A Woman of No Importance*

'Never done nothink to get myself into no trouble, 'cept in not moving on ... But I'm a-moving on now. I'm a-moving on to the berryin ground – that's the move as I'm up to.'
CHARLES DICKENS, *Bleak House* (Jo)

[Her own epitaph] Excuse My Dust.
DOROTHY PARKER, Attrib.

I feel confident I should have been a rebel Angel had the opportunity been mine.

JOHN KEATS, Letter to B. R. Haydon, May 1817

All say, 'How hard it is that we have to die' – a strange complaint to come from the mouths of people who have had to live.

MARK TWAIN, *Pudd'nhead Wilson*

My time has been passed viciously and agreeably; at thirty-one so few years, months, days remain, that 'Carpe diem' is not enough. I have been obliged to crop even the seconds, for who can trust to-morrow? – to-morrow quotha? to-hour, to-minute ...

LORD BYRON, Letter to Hobhouse, 1819

Now I believe courage to be the greatest of human virtues, and the only gift we can impart. ... life is of a hardness that still fairly terrifies me.

VIRGINIA WOOLF, Letter, 1 March 1937

So shalt thou feed on Death, that feeds on men, And Death once dead, there's no more dying then.

WILLIAM SHAKESPEARE, Sonnet 146

If one was to think constantly of death the business of life would stand still.

DR JOHNSON, Attrib.

I fear I have lost the hearing of one ear ... Why should anything go wrong in our bodies? Why should we not be all beautiful? Why should there be decay? – why death? – and, oh, why damnation? the last we get out of by not believing it.
ANTHONY TROLLOPE, Letter, 9 October 1873

The first duty in life is to be as artificial as possible. What the second is, no one has yet discovered.
OSCAR WILDE, *Phrases and Philosophies for the Use of the Young*

Life is monstrous, infinite, illogical, abrupt and poignant.
ROBERT LOUIS STEVENSON, 'A Humble Remonstrance'

I am ready to meet my Maker. Whether my Maker is prepared for the great ordeal of meeting me is another matter.
WINSTON CHURCHILL, Attrib.

One should die quickly, like the Romans, one should be master of one's fate in dying as in living.
D. H. LAWRENCE, *Women in Love*

Life's to me a weary dream,
A dream of ane that never wauks.
ROBERT BURNS, 'Composed in Spring'

In any question why we died,
Tell them, because our fathers lied.
RUDYARD KIPLING, 'Common Form'

Death seems to me as natural a process as birth; inevitable, absolute and final. If, when it happens to me, I find myself in a sort of Odeon ante-room queuing up for an interview with Our Lord, I shall be very surprised indeed ...
Noël Coward, *The Noel Coward Diaries*, 19 March 1955

One may reasonably ask one thing of life, that it should not tear rents in the illusions it creates.
Somerset Maugham, Attrib.

Travel, trouble, music art
A kiss, a frock, a rhyme –
I never said they feed my heart
But still they pass the time.
Dorothy Parker, 'Faute de Mieux'

Time marches on and no word from the Whisker [Laura Waugh]. I hope this means that you are happily engaged or piously in retreat, not that you are dead. If you are dead please be buried in the corner of the field adjoining the village cemetery. Have a small piece cut off & consecrated.
I will design the tomb on my return.
Evelyn Waugh, *Letters*

For me, I sometimes think that life is death,
Rather than life a mere affair of breath.
Lord Byron, *Don Juan*

Twist ye, twine ye! even so
Mingle shades of joy and woe,
Hope and fear, and peace and strife,
In the thread of human life.
SIR WALTER SCOTT, *Guy Mannering*

Is not all life the struggle of experience, naked, unarmed,
timid but immortal, against generalised thought?
W. B. YEATS, Journal, August 1910

Bygones would never be complete bygones till
she was a bygone herself.
THOMAS HARDY, *Tess of the d'Urbervilles*

The past and the future are the two great bournes of human
emotion. They are both conclusive, final. Their beauty is the
beauty of the goal, finished, perfected.
D. H. LAWRENCE, *New Poems*

Why is it that we rejoice at a birth and grieve at a funeral?
It is because we are not the person involved.
MARK TWAIN, *Pudd'nhead Wilson*

There is sadness in coming to the end of anything in life.
Man's instincts cling to the Life that will never end.
LEWIS CARROLL, *Life and Letters*

The Self

Only at his maximum does an individual surpass all his
derivative elements and become purely himself.
D. H. Lawrence, *Fantasia of the Unconscious*

I am certainly not one of those who need to be prodded.
In fact, if anything, I am a prod.
Winston Churchill, Speech in the House of Commons,
11 November 1942

> Given my freedom, I may be a fool to use it,
> but I would be a cad not to.
> Ezra Pound, *Guide to Kulchur*

If we cannot imagine ourselves as different from what we
are, and try to assume that second self, we cannot impose a
discipline upon ourselves though we may accept one from
others. Active virtue, as distinguished from the passive
acceptance of a code, is therefore theatrical, consciously
dramatic, the wearing of a mask.
W. B. Yeats, 'Per Amica Silentia Lunae'

I will not be 'famous', 'great'. I will go on adventuring,
changing, opening my mind and my eyes, refusing to be
stamped and stereotyped.
Virginia Woolf, *A Writer's Diary*, 29 October 1933

I always believe anything anyone tells me about myself –
don't you?
F. Scott Fitzgerald, *The Beautiful and Damned*

I do now want to be independent that I may sin,
but I do want to be independent in my sinning.
ROBERT BURNS, Letter to Mr Cunningham, 11 June 1791

I have been an author for 20 years and an ass for 55.
MARK TWAIN, Attrib.

Chance furnishes me what I need. I am like a man who
stumbles along; my foot strikes something, I bend over and it
is exactly what I want.
JAMES JOYCE, Attrib.

I do not want people to be very agreeable, as it saves me the
trouble of liking them a great deal.
JANE AUSTEN, *Letters*, 24 December 1798

It's not that I want to be a gay dog,
but I want to be a gay dog if I want to.
SOMERSET MAUGHAM, Attrib.

I do not care to be amused – I prefer to be interested.
BENJAMIN DISRAELI, Attrib.

There are three things extremely hard, steel, a diamond,
and to know one's self.
BENJAMIN FRANKLIN, *Poor Richard's Almanack*

I am indeed very wretched, and like all complaining persons I can't help telling you so.

LORD BYRON, Letter to Hobhouse, 1811

At every single moment of one's life one is what one is going to be no less than what one has been.

OSCAR WILDE, *De Profundis*

> I was forced into a measure that no one adopts voluntarily: I was impelled to think. God, was it difficult!
>
> F. SCOTT FITZGERALD, *The Crack-Up*

I demand, and I shall never cease to demand, a greater degree of communication.

EZRA POUND, *Selected Prose*

> I am doomed to be an idler throughout my whole life.
>
> WILLIAM WORDSWORTH, *Letters*

I was never afraid of failure; for I would sooner fail than not be among the greatest.

JOHN KEATS, Letter to J. A. Hessey, October 1818

We are not slaves bound to suffer incessantly unrecorded petty blows on our bent backs. We are not sheep either, following a master. We are creators.

VIRGINIA WOOLF, *The Waves*

My sense of my own importance to the world is relatively small. On the other hand, my sense of my own importance to myself is tremendous. I am all that I have, to work with, to play with, to suffer and to enjoy. It is not the eyes of others that I am wary of, but my own.

NOËL COWARD, *Present Indicative*

I know now that revelation is from the self, but from that age-long memoried self, that shapes the elaborate shell of the mollusc and the child in the womb, that teaches the birds to make their nest; and that genius is a crisis that joins that buried self for certain moments to our trivial daily mind.

W. B. YEATS, *The Trembling of the Veil*

[When asked by a woman sitting next to her at a first night] 'Are you Dorothy Parker?', 'Yes, do you mind?'

DOROTHY PARKER, Attrib.

I do not like photographs, and dislike my own worse than all others.

ANTHONY TROLLOPE, Letter, 15 August 1878

I tell you that as long as I can conceive something better than myself I cannot be easy unless I am striving to bring it into existence or clearing the way for it. That is the law of my life.

GEORGE BERNARD SHAW, *Man and Superman*

We are all worms. But I do believe that I am a glow worm.

WINSTON CHURCHILL, Attrib.

I was born lazy. I am no lazier now than I was forty years ago,
but that is because I reached the limit forty years ago.
You can't go beyond possibility.
MARK TWAIN, Attrib.

I go deeper than 'custom' for my convictions.
W. B. YEATS, *A General Introduction to my Work*

> I am rather frightened by hearing that she wishes to be
> introduced to *me*. If I *am* a wild beast, I cannot help it.
> JANE AUSTEN, *Letters*, 24 May 1813

I never publish anything without great violence to my own
disposition which is to shun, rather than to court, regard.
WILLIAM WORDSWORTH, *Letters*

Outside interests generally mean for me women, liquor or
some form of exhibitionism.
F. SCOTT FITZGERALD, *The Letters*, 7 September 1934

I decline to suffer for what I don't believe in.
EZRA POUND, *Letters*, 1915

The living self has one purpose only: to come into its own
fullness of being, as a tree comes into full blossom, or a bird into
spring beauty, or a tiger into lustre ... The only thing man has
to trust to in coming to himself is his desire and his impulse.
D. H. LAWRENCE, 'Democracy'

No: I intend no introspection. I mark Henry James' sentence:
observe perpetually. Observe the oncome of age.
Observe greed. Observe my own despondency.
By that means it becomes serviceable. Or so I hope.
I insist upon spending my time to the best advantage.
I will go down with my colours flying.
VIRGINIA WOOLF, *A Writer's Diary*, 8 March 1941

I will cut myself a path through the world or perish in the
attempt ... I will carve myself the passage to Grandeur,
but never with Dishonour.
LORD BYRON, Letter to His Mother, 1804

It is not very comfortable to have the gift of being amused at
one's own absurdity.
SOMERSET MAUGHAM, Attrib.

I am of the true Shakespearian type: I understand everything
and everybody, and am nobody and nothing.
GEORGE BERNARD SHAW, Letter to Frank Harris, 20 June 1930

[Interviewer] What do you feel is your worst fault?
[Waugh] Irritability ... with absolutely everything.
Inanimate objects and people, animals, anything.
EVELYN WAUGH, BBC Interview, 20 July 1960

The music in my heart I bore,
Long after it was heard no more.
WILLIAM WORDSWORTH, 'The Solitary Reaper'

No wonder my head hurts, all of Europe fell on it. When I talk, it is like an explosion in an art museum; you have to hunt around for the pieces.
EZRA POUND, *The Caged Panther*

[When asked why he was called 'The Master']
Oh, you know – Jack of all trades, master of none.
NOËL COWARD, Interview with Quentin Crew, *Sunday Mirror*

I like criticism but it must be my way.
MARK TWAIN, *Autobiography*

You have got two beautiful bad examples for parents. Just do everything we didn't do and you will be perfectly safe.
F. SCOTT FITZGERALD, *The Letters*, December 1940

Every life is many days, day after day. We walk through ourselves, meeting robbers, ghosts, giants, old men, young men, wives, widows, brothers-in-love, but always meeting ourselves.
JAMES JOYCE, *Ulysses*

I think I may boast myself to be, with all possible vanity, the most unlearned and uninformed female who ever dared to be an authoress.
JANE AUSTEN, *Letters*, 11 December 1815

Index of Contributors